CHINA POLICY

BY A. DOAK BARNETT

Communist Economic Strategy: The Rise of Mainland China
(1959)

Communist China and Asia: Challenge to American Policy
(1960)

Communist China in Perspective
(1962)

*Communist Strategies in Asia: A Comparative Analysis
of Governments and Parties*
(editor, 1963)

China on the Eve of Communist Takeover
(1963)

Communist China: The Early Years, 1949–1955
(1964)

The United States and China in World Affairs
(editor of manuscript by Robert Blum; published posthumously, 1966)

China after Mao
(1967)

Cadres, Bureaucracy, and Political Power in Communist China
(with a contribution by Ezra Vogel, 1967)

Chinese Communist Politics in Action
(editor, 1969)

The United States and China: The Next Decade
(editor, with Edwin O. Reischauer, 1970)

A New U.S. Policy toward China
(Brookings, 1971)

Uncertain Passage: China's Transition to the Post-Mao Era
(Brookings, 1974)

The United States, China, and Arms Control
(with Ralph N. Clough, Morton H. Halperin, and Jerome H. Kahan;
Brookings, 1975)

China Policy: Old Problems and New Challenges
(Brookings, 1977)

China and the Major Powers in East Asia
(Brookings, 1977)

A. Doak Barnett

CHINA POLICY

Old Problems and New Challenges

THE BROOKINGS INSTITUTION
Washington, D.C.

Copyright © 1977 by
THE BROOKINGS INSTITUTION
1775 Massachusetts Avenue, N.W., Washington, D.C. 20036

Library of Congress Cataloging in Publication Data:

Barnett, A   Doak.
   China policy, old problems and new challenges.
   Includes bibliographical references and index.
     1. United States—Relations (general) with China.
   2. China—Relations (general) with the United States.
   3. United States—Foreign relations—1945–
   I. Title.
   E183.8.C5B22   301.29′73′051   76-51538
   ISBN 0-8157-0822-X
   ISBN 0-8157-0821-1 pbk.

1 2 3 4 5 6 7 8 9

To my daughter

MARTHA JEANNE BARNETT

THE BROOKINGS INSTITUTION is an independent organization devoted to nonpartisan research, education, and publication in economics, government, foreign policy, and the social sciences generally. Its principal purposes are to aid in the development of sound public policies and to promote public understanding of issues of national importance.

The Institution was founded on December 8, 1927, to merge the activities of the Institute for Government Research, founded in 1916, the Institute of Economics, founded in 1922, and the Robert Brookings Graduate School of Economics and Government, founded in 1924.

The Board of Trustees is responsible for the general administration of the Institution, while the immediate direction of the policies, program, and staff is vested in the President, assisted by an advisory committee of the officers and staff. The bylaws of the Institution state: "It is the function of the Trustees to make possible the conduct of scientific research, and publication, under the most favorable conditions, and to safeguard the independence of the research staff in the pursuit of their studies and in the publication of the results of such studies. It is not a part of their function to determine, control, or influence the conduct of particular investigations or the conclusions reached."

The President bears final responsibility for the decision to publish a manuscript as a Brookings book. In reaching his judgment on the competence, accuracy, and objectivity of each study, the President is advised by the director of the appropriate research program and weighs the views of a panel of expert outside readers who report to him in confidence on the quality of the work. Publication of a work signifies that it is deemed a competent treatment worthy of public consideration but does not imply endorsement of conclusions or recommendations.

The Institution maintains its position of neutrality on issues of public policy in order to safeguard the intellectual freedom of the staff. Hence interpretations or conclusions in Brookings publications should be understood to be solely those of the authors and should not be attributed to the Institution, to its trustees, officers, or other staff members, or to the organizations that support its research.

Foreword

THE IMPROVEMENT of U.S.-China relations, Doak Barnett wrote in 1971, must be viewed as "a gradual, cautious process of mutual accommodation." A few months before President Richard M. Nixon's visit to China in February 1972, Barnett, in *A New U.S. Policy toward China*, called for basic changes in American policy. Since then American policy has changed, and relations between Washington and Peking have improved, yet many difficult issues and problems lie ahead. Barnett's warning that it "might take much of the coming decade to work toward a new pattern of interactions" has been borne out.

In this book, Barnett argues that there is no basis for complacency about the relationship developed since the Shanghai communiqué of 1972. He maintains that there could be retrogression and damage to U.S. interests unless there is further movement soon toward normalization of U.S.-China ties. But normalization will require harder decisions than those made in 1972. Barnett defines the immediate issues and offers prescriptions for what he believes would be a realistic U.S. policy.

Barnett also discusses some of the major long-run issues and their bearing on U.S. policy. He examines trade and other economic relations; scientific, technological, and cultural exchanges; future U.S.-China military-security relations and arms control; U.S. China policy in the context of the East Asian interests of the Soviet Union and Japan; and areas of potential conflict such as Korea and Southeast Asia.

Doak Barnett was born in Shanghai and has studied China for the past thirty years. He has had broad experience in government, journalism, and academic affairs, and is the author of or contributor to three previous Brookings books on China and U.S. policy. He is grateful to Alice M. Carroll, who edited the manuscript of this book, and to Florence Robinson, who prepared the index.

Financial support for this study was provided by the Rockefeller Foundation and the Office of External Research of the U.S. Department of State. As in all Brookings books, the views expressed here are those of the author, and should not be ascribed to the Rockefeller Foundation, to the Department of State, or to the trustees, officers, or other staff members of the Brookings Institution.

GILBERT Y. STEINER
Acting President

December 1976
Washington, D.C.

Contents

I

U.S.-China Relations
in the 1970s

THE OPENING of relations between the United States and the People's Republic of China in 1972 was a watershed, both in their bilateral dealings and in broader East Asian affairs. It ended two decades of bitterly hostile Sino-American confrontation and started the process of "normalizing" U.S.-China relations. In regional terms it marked the emergence of a new and very different pattern of four-power relationships in East Asia.

The changes, important as they are, have merely initiated a process of mutual accommodation, however; and as is often the case in international relations, the solution of certain problems has created new sets of issues. The ties between Washington and Peking are still limited and fairly fragile, and it remains to be seen whether the normalizing process can even be carried through to establishment of full diplomatic relations. There is no guarantee of success; instead of further progress toward improved relations, there could be retrogression. If and when full diplomatic links can be established, major problems will still lie ahead. The task of expanding the U.S.-China relationship, and the search for a new basis for agreements or understandings on a wide range of problems vital to peace and security in East Asia, will be long and difficult. Although the four powers in the region—Japan and the Soviet Union as well as the United States and China—could create a new and more stable equilibrium in East Asia, they also could pursue policies that would result in renewed tension, instability, and conflict.

Continuing uncertainty about the future should not, however, obscure the importance of the already far-reaching consequences of the Sino-American détente. The unexpected decision to initiate new contacts between high officials represented a bold initiative by both sides, and Henry Kissinger's secret trip to Peking in 1971 had an enormous impact internationally. This was in part because for more than two decades U.S.-China hostility had been widely accepted as one of the givens of international relations.

The deep antagonism between Washington and Peking that began in the fifties had been intensified by a series of military and political conflicts and crises on China's periphery. The resulting mutual hostility seemed likely to last indefinitely. Not only were the two countries divided by an enormous ideological, political, economic, and cultural chasm; the bitterness resulting from the Korean War seemed to ensure continuing conflicts of American and Chinese interests wherever these came in contact in East Asia, from Korea to Taiwan to Southeast Asia.[1]

The Korean War, more than anything else, set the framework for U.S.-China confrontation throughout the 1950s and 1960s. One of the consequences of the war was the renewal of American support for the Chinese Nationalist regime on Taiwan, from which Washington had largely disengaged its interests in late 1949 and early 1950. This reinvolved the United States in China's civil war.

As a result of the conflict in Korea, each country saw the other as posing a serious threat to its basic security interests, in China's case to its own national security as well as that of its immediate Communist neighbors, in the U.S. case to the security of noncommunist friends and allies in Asia. After the war, Washington pursued a policy designed to contain, isolate, and exert pressure on China to try to weaken it, while Peking relentlessly attacked and attempted to undermine the U.S. position throughout East Asia. Gradually and subtly, however, the perceptions of both American and Chinese leaders of the international situation in general and of each other's threat in particular began to change, in the 1960s. The most important factor in this change was the steady widening

---

1. See, for background, Foster Rhea Dulles, *American Policy Toward Communist China, The Historical Record: 1949–1969* (Crowell, 1972); Roderick MacFarquhar and others, *Sino-American Relations, 1949–1971* (Praeger, 1972); A. Doak Barnett, *Communist China and Asia: Challenge to American Policy* (Harper, 1960); Kenneth T. Young, *Negotiating with the Chinese Communists: The United States Experience, 1953–1963* (McGraw-Hill, 1968); Robert Blum, *The United States and China in World Affairs* (McGraw-Hill, 1966); and *China and U.S. Foreign Policy*, 2nd ed. (Washington: Congressional Quarterly, Inc., 1973).

of the Sino-Soviet split that had begun in the 1950s. The conflict between Peking and Moscow escalated greatly in the 1960s, and was transformed from an essentially political dispute into an open military confrontation in the face of the Russians' major military buildup around China's borders from 1965 on. By the late 1960s, Peking's leaders were seriously concerned by the military threat to their country's security.

Meanwhile, as U.S. leaders came to grasp more fully the reality of the Sino-Soviet conflict and its far-reaching international significance, the "China threat" was gradually downgraded. Washington began to realize also that Peking was generally more prudent in its international actions than its ideological rhetoric implied, and that China's domestic preoccupations, especially during the Cultural Revolution in 1966–68, as well as its limited military capabilities, imposed severe constraints on its foreign policy. Moreover, as the passions aroused by the Korean War cooled, American public opinion toward China slowly moderated. All of these factors induced the U.S. government to move toward a more flexible posture toward China, although it still did little to change its concrete policies.

Conflict by proxy continued as Washington and Peking gave strong support to opposite sides in the bitter struggle in Vietnam, and the danger of direct clashes between them rose again after the United States intervened on a large scale in the South, with its own forces, in 1964–65. But despite the escalation of fighting, both governments acted to prevent another U.S.-China conflict such as had occurred in Korea, and their mutual restraint limited the dangers inherent in the situation.

The U.S.-China Opening

The first steps toward active exploration of the possibility of a U.S.-China opening took place in the late 1960s, at a time when Sino-Soviet relations had reached their nadir and when the United States made its first moves toward eventual military disengagement from Vietnam. During 1968–69, for the first time since 1949, both Washington and Peking, each for its own reasons, saw compelling reasons to try to establish a new U.S.-China relationship.

On the Chinese side, national security considerations, above all, dictated the adoption of a new general foreign policy strategy. Peking's leaders, and in particular Chairman Mao Tse-tung, concluded that the

Soviet Union had replaced the United States as the main military threat to China and therefore had become China's "principal enemy." In light of the Soviet buildup around China, Moscow's invasion of Czechoslovakia in 1968 aroused intense apprehension in Peking about possible Soviet intervention in China, and the Sino-Soviet border clashes in 1969 brought the two countries close to war. Despite some internal opposition, Mao and Premier Chou En-lai concluded that they should explore the possibility of links to the United States, which might create a new counterweight to restrain Moscow, even if this required certain compromises that Peking had previously been unwilling to consider.

Apparently, China's top leaders were now convinced that American power in Asia had peaked and was destined to decline, thereby reducing the likelihood of a direct American military threat to China. Their increasing concern, especially after the 1969 meeting between President Richard Nixon and Premier Eisaku Sato, that the United States might encourage Japan to rearm and assume a regional military role provided a further argument for establishing new ties with both Washington and Tokyo.

On the U.S. side, President Lyndon Johnson had made a first move in 1968 toward the withdrawal of U.S. military forces from Vietnam, and, following the elections that fall, President Nixon and his principal foreign policy adviser Henry Kissinger recognized that American public opinion compelled them to move further down that road. It was evident that this would involve dangers and that if it were possible to establish new contacts with China this might facilitate the process and reduce the risks, not only of military disengagement from Vietnam itself but also of the broader reduction in the U.S. military presence in Asia which the President proposed in his so-called Nixon Doctrine in 1969.

Equally or more important, Nixon and Kissinger hoped to achieve greater leverage in dealing with Moscow, which they viewed as Washington's primary adversary. Despite counterarguments by skeptics in Washington, they believed that improved U.S.-China relations could impose new constraints on the Russians and might push them toward greater compromise and détente. The earlier changes in U.S. public opinion and downgrading of the China threat paved the way for policy changes, and Nixon's invulnerability to attack from the Republican party's right wing gave him a flexibility in considering China policy options that his Democratic predecessors had felt they lacked.

In sum, by 1968–69 certain important military, geopolitical, strategic interests argued for a new Sino-American relationship. Leaders in Washington and Peking began to probe each other's intentions to explore what might be possible. In November 1968, soon after Moscow's invasion of Czechoslovakia and on the eve of the start of the new administration in Washington, Peking called for the reopening of the long-stalled U.S.-China talks at Warsaw and proposed that the two countries reach agreement on "five principles of coexistence."[2] Soon after he assumed office, President Nixon ordered a general review of China policy, and in mid-1969 he began unilaterally taking a series of small but symbolic steps to reduce U.S. restrictions on travel and trade with China. Before the end of the year, the United States had ended active naval patrolling in the Taiwan Strait.

The Warsaw talks were reopened, after some delay, but the most important mutual probing took place through varied intermediaries, including the French, Rumanians, and Pakistanis.[3] The process was punctuated by new crises in Vietnam, plus the invasions of Cambodia and Laos, which resulted in temporary setbacks. But in late 1970 and early 1971, Peking, apparently convinced that the United States was really disengaging from Vietnam, indicated both publicly and privately that it would welcome a visit to China by a high-level emissary. Kissinger's secret trip followed, and it prepared the way for President Nixon's summit meetings with Chairman Mao and Premier Chou in February 1972. These produced the Shanghai communiqué, which defined a very new framework for U.S.-China relations.

The drama of the President's trip to Peking maximized the immediate impact of the opening of U.S.-China relations. The two countries demonstrated in a highly visible way that they wished to end the two-decade-old pattern of Sino-American confrontation and that, even though they could not immediately find a basis for establishing full diplomatic relations, they were ready at least to begin the process of normalization. It was immediately clear that a new configuration of big-power relations in East Asia was in the making, and every country in the region was compelled to start reassessing its situation and adjusting its policies to fit the new situation. The Soviet Union stepped up its efforts to cement ties with India and influence Japan, its calls for détente with the United States, and its attempts to compete against Chinese influence generally. Japan moved rapidly to establish full diplomatic relations with China and

2. *Peking Review*, Nov. 28, 1968, p. 31.
3. See Marvin Kalb and Bernard Kalb, *Kissinger* (Little, Brown, 1974), pp. 216 ff.

adopted a posture of "equidistance" in dealing with Peking and Moscow. The smaller nations in East Asia began, individually, to adjust their policies to the realities of the new four-power balance in the region.

Although unresolved differences regarding Taiwan still prevented full diplomatic ties between the two countries, their leaders stated in the Shanghai communiqué that they would "stay in contact through various channels, including the sending of a senior U.S. representative to Peking from time to time," and they called for efforts to "facilitate the further development of . . . contacts and exchanges" and "the progressive development of trade."[4]

Immediately thereafter, new U.S.-China links of various sorts were established, more rapidly than was generally expected. For a time Kissinger virtually commuted to Peking, averaging two visits a year. Then, in a surprising move, the United States and China agreed in 1973 to establish in each other's capitals so-called liaison offices, which were embassies in all but name. Since Peking had for years adamantly opposed the idea of maintaining diplomatic representation in the capital of any country that recognized the Republic of China on Taiwan, this represented an important compromise. Nonofficial U.S.-China exchanges also developed fairly rapidly, and trade skyrocketed, rising to a peak of almost $1 billion in 1974.

In many respects, 1972 and 1973 were honeymoon years in the new relationship. Peking stressed the positive whenever possible, and in direct contacts with the Americans the Chinese generally avoided making an issue of unresolved problems. On the American side, public opinion underwent one of the great pendulum swings characteristic of American attitudes toward China, and unreasoning hostility was replaced by uncritical euphoria. Many Americans assumed that full diplomatic relations would be established easily and soon and that the broader process of expanding ties would be relatively simple.

A Holding Pattern

By late 1973 and early 1974 there were signs that the normalization process had begun to slow down, and thereafter observers began to talk

4. For the text of the communiqué, see *Department of State Bulletin*, Mar. 20, 1972, pp. 435–38.

of a "cooling," and a "plateau" in the relationship. In fact, the relationship entered a holding pattern, and by the time of Chairman Mao's death there had been little significant movement.

Such a sequence of developments is not unique. Relations between the People's Republic of China and many countries have gone through an initial period of euphoria, immediately following normalization of relations, after which old and new problems have come to the fore. But the U.S. case is special, in part because China's relations with the United States are more important than its relations with most other countries, and in part because full diplomatic ties will be particularly difficult to establish because of the Taiwan problem. The original U.S.-China opening and the signing of the Shanghai communiqué were possible because both sides were willing, in effect, to lay the Taiwan problem temporarily aside, making some compromises but not resolving the fundamental issues. Basic differences on Taiwan continue, and they still pose the crucial obstacle to normal relations, especially from Peking's perspective.

Peking's leaders seem to have decided around the beginning of 1974 to exert subtle pressure to induce further changes in American policy toward Taiwan. While still viewing the Soviet Union as the major threat to their interests, worldwide, they may have concluded that the danger of Russian military attack had diminished to a degree, permitting somewhat greater flexibility in China's policies toward both Moscow and Washington. By 1973, China had emplaced a number of operational nuclear missiles and thus had acquired a nuclear deterrent of sorts; it began publicly to play down the Soviet military threat to itself, stressing instead the danger posed by Moscow to Europe.[5]

On a diplomatic level, the changes became evident in negotiations with Washington on an "assets and claims" agreement (to settle long-standing mutual claims) that had seemed close to success in 1973; Peking delayed taking the final steps required to consummate it. In nonofficial exchanges, the Chinese showed increasing sensitivity on the Taiwan issue,

---

5. In May 1973 Premier Chou En-lai told Marquis Childs that he was confident that "a Soviet strike across the northern border, so long a major threat, has been deterred" (*Washington Post*, May 26, 1973). By August he was arguing that the Russians were "making a feint to the East (i.e. China) while attacking in the West (i.e. Europe)" (*Peking Review*, Sept. 7, 1973, p. 22). As of 1974 it was estimated that the Chinese had acquired 200 to 300 nuclear weapons and had emplaced about 50 operational medium-range ballistic missiles and 20 to 30 intermediate-range ballistic missiles (International Institute for Strategic Studies, *The Military Balance, 1974–1975* [London: IISS, 1974], pp. 48–49).

and they began raising problems that they had been willing to overlook in 1972–73. When Americans proposed expanding and improving exchanges, the Chinese indicated that the establishment of full diplomatic ties should come first. In 1975, Sino-American trade dropped sharply, to roughly half the 1974 level. Although increased Chinese grain production had reduced Peking's need for food imports, political considerations were obviously involved; in discussing trade, as well as exchanges, the Chinese indicated that the lack of fully normalized relations inhibited further development.

Peking clearly continued to hope for further U.S. steps toward normalization, however. Until 1974, it may have anticipated that this would be possible before the end of the Nixon administration, and it seemed to believe that its subtle pressures were necessary to help the process along.

The U.S. government, on its part, continued taking small steps to demonstrate its commitment to implement the Shanghai communiqué. In 1974, with the administration's blessing, the U.S. Congress repealed the 1955 Formosa Resolution, and Washington reduced the number of American military men on Taiwan to under four thousand (by the end of 1976 the number had been cut to close to two thousand). These moves may have been less than wholly convincing to Peking, however; not only was Washington slow in completing its total military withdrawal from Taiwan, it made some decisions that Peking unquestionably viewed as retrogressive. For example, it appointed a senior American diplomat as its new ambassador to Taiwan, permitted the Nationalists to open two new consulates in the United States, and increased credit-financed sales of American military equipment to the Nationalist regime. Peking's subtle pressures may, in part, have been in reaction to these U.S. steps.

From 1974 on, in any case, a number of major developments complicated the process of normalization and made delay seem unavoidable. The Watergate crisis, culminating in Nixon's resignation, seriously disrupted the policy process in Washington. Although his appointed successor, Gerald Ford, agreed in late 1974 to hold a second U.S.-China summit meeting in Peking a year later, the change in leadership in Washington reduced the possibility of major U.S. policy initiatives in the immediate future. Then, in 1975, the international context in East Asia changed drastically. The rapid collapse of the noncommunist regimes in Vietnam and Cambodia in the spring created an atmosphere of instability and uncertainty which convinced U.S. leaders that their most urgent task was to reassure Asians that the United States did not intend to withdraw from Asia. Shortly thereafter, following the death of Chiang Kai-shek, prominent members of President Ford's own party began publicly warning against changes in U.S. policy that might weaken Taiwan's position.

Within the U.S. government, there were differing views on whether Washington should try to move soon toward full diplomatic relations, and if so what further compromises regarding Taiwan would be necessary, and acceptable. Those urging rapid normalization warned that the passing of Mao and Chou, both of whose health was fading, would introduce many new uncertainties. However, domestic political factors in the United States, as well as the international atmosphere, bolstered the arguments of those favoring delay. The presidential elections were little more than a year away, and it became clear that Ford would face a serious challenge in his bid for renomination from the right wing of his party; further compromise on Taiwan could make him vulnerable to political attacks from that quarter.

It appears that Peking's leaders decided in the spring of 1975 that it was unrealistic to expect further movement toward normalization of U.S.-China relations until after the American presidential elections. They may even have concluded that the sudden changes in Vietnam made a short delay desirable. There was increasing evidence of uncertainty in Peking about Washington's ability or willingness to serve as an effective counterweight to the Russians, which had been the primary Chinese goal in establishing a new relationship with the United States.

In the late spring of 1975 the Chinese reverted, publicly, to an attitude of patience toward the Taiwan problem and emphasized almost entirely the need for stronger opposition to the Soviet threat. Perhaps concerned that President Ford's trip might be canceled, they stressed their interest in having him come, but at the same time their criticism of U.S.-Soviet détente became increasingly open and strident.

President Ford did visit China, on schedule, in late 1975. The visit was of symbolic significance, but little was accomplished to move Sino-American relations forward. Both sides demonstrated their continuing recognition of certain common geopolitical and security interests, in particular vis-à-vis the Soviet Union, and both indicated a desire to maintain the U.S.-China relationship at the existing level. But because the trip produced no substantive improvement in Sino-American ties, it also highlighted the obstacles that remained to normalizing those ties. After that, U.S.-China relations remained on dead center.

New Political Uncertainties

Uncertainty about future relations has increased as a result of domestic political developments in both the United States and China. In early 1976 the Chinese succession struggle entered a critical final stage. This struggle had been virtually continuous since the Cultural Revolution upheaval of the latter half of the 1960s. At that time, Mao purged his principal political opponents, and Lin Piao emerged as his designated heir. However, in 1971, Mao and Lin clashed, and reportedly Lin died in an air crash while fleeing the country. Immediately after Lin's death China's basic problem was to restore order, rebuild the top leadership, and evolve a set of workable domestic and foreign policies. Although Mao retained his unchallengeable position at the top of China's hierarchy, he withdrew increasingly to the background, and Chou En-lai, despite his own declining health, played a crucial role in shaping the leadership group that emerged and the generally pragmatic policies that were publicly articulated and legitimized by the National People's Congress in 1975. Chou helped to bring back to power many experienced party leaders who had been purged during the Cultural Revolution; one of them, Teng Hsiao-p'ing, appeared destined to succeed him as premier and to carry on his pragmatic policies.

However, Chou's death in early 1976 precipitated a strong counterattack by China's "radicals," and the compromises he had arranged fell apart. The radicals succeeded, with Mao's backing, in purging Teng, and Hua Kuo-feng, a little-known leader, became premier; he was also designated first vice chairman of the party, second only to Mao in the hierarchy.

China's succession crisis reached a climax in September 1976 when Mao died. Within a month, Hua Kuo-feng emerged as party chairman after a brief but intense power struggle. Earlier, Hua had generally been viewed as the compromise choice of competing groups of "radicals" and "pragmatists" in China's leadership, but he now appeared to align himself clearly with the country's civilian and military pragmatists. Mao's wife and the other leading radicals were purged and denounced. This could presage a decisive and extremely important shift in the direction of China's policies, but it is still too early to say definitely. It remains to be seen whether Hua will be able to consolidate his position as party chairman, what kind of leadership group he will head, and what changes in China's domestic and foreign policies will occur. Mao's death and the succession inevitably introduce a period of great uncertainty in China.

For more than a decade the succession struggle in China had been fueled not only by power rivalries but also by basic differences over policy. Although the main debates have focused on domestic issues, there have been significant differences over foreign policy too. These widened following the major foreign policy shifts—including the opening to the United States—engineered by Mao and Chou in the late 1960s and early 1970s.[6]

The most divisive differences on foreign policy have been over policy toward the United States and the Soviet Union. China's radicals were critical from the start of the opening to the United States. Hostile to both Washington and Moscow on ideological grounds, they were predisposed to advocate a hard line toward both. Their indictment of the U.S.-China opening stressed that it could seriously compromise China's goal of self-reliance and expose the country to subversive ideological and political influences.[7]

Doubts about Peking's current policy toward the United States have not been confined to China's radicals, however. Others have become increasingly impatient, since the 1972 signing of the Shanghai communiqué, and some doubtless believe that Peking has given too much and gotten too little in regard to the Taiwan issue, which appears almost as far from final resolution as ever. Certain pragmatic leaders also seem to believe a more flexible policy to protect China's security might be better than maintaining a totally hostile posture toward Moscow, hoping that Washington can keep it in check.

6. See testimony of Harry Harding, Jr., A. Doak Barnett, and others, in *United States-China Relations: The Process of Normalization of Relations*, Hearings before a Special Subcommittee on Investigations of the House Committee on International Relations (Government Printing Office, 1976).

7. A 1973 document, "Outline of Education on Situation for Companies," used to indoctrinate troops, indicated that there had been doubts and opposition to the Sino-American opening from the start. It denounced "some comrades" who "slander and vilify us, saying that our talks with the United States meant a 'collusion between China and the United States', an 'alliance with the United States against the Soviet Union', etc." (the text, reproduced in *Issues and Studies* [Taipei], June 1974, pp. 90 ff., and July 1974, pp. 99 ff., was obtained by the Republic of China's intelligence apparatus and is probably authentic). Attacks by radicals on compromise of the principle of self-reliance increased during 1976, especially after Chou En-lai's death (see Chin Feng, "Down with Underestimating of Oneself," *Selections from People's Republic of China Magazines*, 74-15, no. 789, Sept. 20, 1974, pp. 1–3). For an analysis of the debate, see Victor Zorza, *Washington Post*, Aug. 27, 1974.

Criticism of Mao's policy toward the Soviet Union can be traced as far back as the 1950s, and the critics have included some of China's top military leaders. While Mao was obsessed with the danger of subversive Soviet influence in China, as well as with Moscow's external threat, and for years advocated an implacably hostile confrontational posture toward Moscow, his major critics appear to have believed, on essentially pragmatic grounds, that a less hostile policy might better serve China's security interests. Today there are probably few leaders in Peking who believe that close Sino-Soviet relations are now possible. Most probably agree that China will long face a Soviet threat. But as recently as 1975 there were hints that some believe the best way to defuse that threat is by adopting a more flexible and compromising posture.[8]

In the summer of 1976 there were also hints that some Chinese leaders favored a harder line on the Taiwan issue. In conversations with Americans, they suggested that Peking might be compelled once again to try to solve the Taiwan problem by force if there were no further progress toward a political resolution of the issue.[9] Even though the Communists are obviously not preparing for military action now, their statements were a departure from Peking's earlier stress on moderation and patience. They may have been reacting against American political statements and actions during 1975-76 that suggested a strengthening of U.S.-Taiwan links. Or they may have been trying to strengthen the Chinese bargaining position in anticipation of further negotiations in 1977 concerning full normalization of relations. It is also possible, however, that some Chinese were pressing for a harder line toward the United States—it is conceivable that individual radical leaders were working to upset the process of normalization.

Although major shifts in Peking's policy toward either Moscow or Washington seemed unlikely before Mao's death, or before Peking could probe the intentions of the next U.S. administration, with both Mao and Chou gone the possibility of change is greater. It will increase if the new administration in Washington gives no evidence, in 1977, of a willingness to take further steps toward full normalization of relations.

It is very possible that new leaders in Peking may begin cautiously to explore the possibilities for reducing Sino-Soviet tensions. The legacy

8. Those who favor a more compromising policy toward Moscow are attacked in An Miao, "Confucianist Capitulationism and Traitor Lin Piao," *Survey of the People's Republic of China Press*, no. 5921 (Aug. 22, 1975), pp. 171-80.

9. *Washington Post*, Aug. 12, 1976, and *New York Times*, Aug. 12, 1976.

of a decade and a half of Sino-Soviet conflict makes it difficult to conceive of any far-reaching rapprochement in the foreseeable future, yet a gradual and limited Sino-Soviet détente, comparable in some respects to the United States' interactions with China and the Soviet Union in recent years, might evolve, if Moscow's leaders are willing to be more flexible. The impact of a limited Sino-Soviet détente on U.S.-China relations and U.S. interests in East Asia as a whole would depend on the context in which it occurred. If Washington-Peking ties had already been reasonably consolidated, the damage would be limited; there might even be some desirable effects. Washington would probably lose, it is true, some of the leverage it now enjoys in dealing with both the Chinese and the Russians, and Moscow might believe it had a somewhat freer hand than at present in dealing with the West in Europe. On the other hand, reduced Sino-Soviet tensions might also remove one obstacle to efforts to increase stability in areas such as Korea and Southeast Asia.

If, however, a process of Sino-Soviet détente were to begin while U.S.-China relations are still fragile, the consequences might be much more adverse. Even though it seems unlikely that pragmatic leaders in Peking will wish to return to the kind of confrontational U.S.-China relationship of the 1950s and 1960s, they might well decide to exert greater pressures on Taiwan and perhaps to adopt a more militant posture toward areas such as Korea and Southeast Asia. The result could be not only a deterioration in the limited relationship that now exists between the United States and China, but also increased anxiety and tension elsewhere in Asia. Conceivably, fear of closer Sino-Soviet cooperation could exert increased pressure on the United States (and Japan) to compromise with China on key issues (including those relating to Taiwan) on terms less favorable than those possible now. The problems of creating a stable equilibrium in East Asia would almost certainly increase.

In the United States, the new uncertainties about China policy are of a different kind. There is no evidence of any strong political opposition to the Washington-Peking ties that have been established so far. In 1974, Kissinger could honestly say that "no policy of this Administration has had greater bipartisan support than the normalization of relations with the People's Republic."[10] Public opinion polls indicate an overwhelming majority of Americans support a policy of normalization, and many political leaders in both parties continue to endorse it. In mid-1976 the

10. Press release, National Committee on United States-China Relations, June 3, 1974.

Democratic nominee for President, Jimmy Carter, urged further steps in that direction, and the Democratic party platform advocated "early movement toward normalizing diplomatic relations in the context of a peaceful resolution of the future of Taiwan."[11] Republican Senate Minority Leader Hugh Scott, on his return from a trip to China, asserted that Carter's statements showed there is "very wide support for movement toward normalization of relations," and he proposed that "early in 1977 we should press the process of cutting this Gordian knot" (i.e., overcoming the obstacles to normalization).[12] He also urged that Taiwan play a positive role in the search for peaceful compromise solutions.

But there have also been signs since 1975 of new political opposition to the kind of compromises regarding Taiwan that will doubtless be required to make possible full normalization of U.S. relations with Peking. Senator Barry Goldwater, at the time of Chiang Kai-shek's funeral in April 1975, criticized the administration for its "shabby treatment of a former ally." He warned that if the administration was considering withdrawal of recognition from the Nationalist regime, "I can assure the Secretary of State and the President that this will not be accomplished without strong opposition from myself and other Americans."[13] A month later House Minority Leader John Rhodes asserted that no steps would be taken soon to further loosen ties with Taiwan, "if President Ford wants to be renominated by the Republican Party."[14] And in February 1976, Ronald Reagan, President Ford's main challenger in his own party, declared that the United States "should not abandon Taiwan to improve relations with China," and he warned against the consequences of letting the Chinese succeed in "talking us into abandoning an ally and violating a treaty."[15]

There were also other signs indicating subtle shifts in public opinion that might make further compromise by Washington on the Taiwan issue difficult. In the House over two hundred signatures were obtained for the so-called Mathis resolution which urged the U.S. government "while engaged in the lessening of tension with the People's Republic of China, to do nothing to compromise the freedom of our friend and

11. *Newsweek*, Aug. 30, 1976, p. 25.
12. *New York Times*, Aug. 12, 1976.
13. Press release, office of Barry Goldwater, Republican senator from Arizona, April 11, 1975.
14. *New York Times*, May 10, 1975.
15. Ibid., Feb. 14, 1976.

ally, the Republic of China and its people."[16] Editorials in some leading newspapers took positions indicating a reduced inclination to compromise on the Taiwan issue. In June 1976, for example, the *New York Times* argued that "the future of 14 million Taiwanese, who do not want to be absorbed by the Communist mainland, would become problematical if the United States withdraws its backing"; and it talked about the dangers of "the beginning of a slippery slope."[17] Two months later, however, it backtracked, stating that "there is no major problem now in adopting the 'Japanese formula'—downgrading diplomatic relations with Taipei to achieve full diplomatic relations with Peking," adding that a prerequisite for abrogation of the U.S. defense treaty with Taiwan should be the requirement that "Peking refrain from open threats of force and tacitly accept viable substitute arrangements."[18]

Several public opinion polls taken in the period 1974–76 showed that a large number of Americans, while supporting existing Washington-Peking ties and in general favoring further steps toward normalization, also incline toward policies on the Taiwan question that would lead to a permanent "two Chinas" arrangement. In 1975, for example, a Gallup poll indicated that while 65 percent of those polled favored "establishing diplomatic relations with mainland China," 70 percent favored "continuing relations with Nationalist China."[19] And in 1976 a Foreign Policy Association survey showed greater support for "a policy looking toward the eventual independence of Taiwan" than for any other single policy option.[20]

The resurfacing of such views, and especially the statements made by men such as Reagan, Goldwater, and Rhodes, clearly was a significant factor inhibiting Ford and his administration from considering further steps toward establishing full diplomatic ties with Peking during 1975–76. These views were reflected in the Republican party platform, which, while it supported contacts, trade, and normalized relations with China, also urged the U.S. government to honor its "commitments, such as the mutual defense treaty" with Taiwan.[21]

16. H. Con. Res. 360, 94:1 (1975).

17. *New York Times*, June 17, 1976.

18. Ibid., Aug. 9, 1976.

19. *A Gallup Study of Public Attitudes Toward Nations in the World* (Princeton, N.J.: Gallup Organization, Inc., October 1975).

20. Foreign Policy Association, *Great Decisions '76 Opinion Ballots*, news release, June 30, 1976.

21. *Newsweek*, Aug. 30, 1976, p. 25.

The predisposition of many Americans to continue dealing with both Peking and Taipei on some kind of two-Chinas basis is understandable. Ideally, this might be the best of all possible solutions from the U.S. point of view, *if* it were acceptable to the parties involved and therefore feasible. Today, however, it does not appear to be a realistic policy option, above all because Peking continues adamantly to insist that if the United States wishes to establish full diplomatic relations with the People's Republic of China, it must sever formal diplomatic ties with the Republic of China on Taiwan. Having maintained this position unyieldingly for a quarter century, it is not likely to abandon it now. In the Shanghai communiqué the United States implicitly pledged that it would not promote any formal two-Chinas solution or support independence for Taiwan. If Washington were to backtrack on this, the results would almost certainly reverse the whole process of normalization.

The United States must, therefore, face up to some difficult policy choices in the period immediately ahead. While it cannot and should not "abandon" Taiwan, it cannot continue to deal with Taiwan on the same basis as in the past if full normalization of relations with Peking is to be achieved. And if full normalization is not achieved, Peking could well reassess its policies and move in new directions in its policy toward either Washington or Moscow or both, with consequences that could damage U.S. interests. Even protracted delay is likely to create new risks, since Peking's posture of patience may not last very long after the change of administration in Washington in 1977.

In the 1950s and 1960s it might have been possible, despite Peking's opposition, to create conditions that could have made a two-Chinas policy feasible. If the United States, with the Nationalists' support or acquiescence, had energetically pushed for representation of both Chinas in the United Nations, there would have been substantial international backing for the idea, and Peking would have been under considerable pressure to accommodate to it. But the Nationalists refused to countenance the idea, and Washington did not move explicitly in this direction until it was too late to test its feasibility.

The situation changed, fundamentally, when the People's Republic displaced the Republic of China in the United Nations and when the overwhelming majority of nations severed their ties with the Nationalist regime and established diplomatic relations with Peking. Since 1971 there has been no realistic basis on which Washington could pursue a successful two-Chinas policy. If the United States were to move in this direction now, it would be virtually alone; in effect, it would be choosing relations with Taiwan *instead* of relations with Peking. Perhaps the situation could change in the long run, but this is the reality that Washington will face in the years immediately ahead.

The need now, therefore, is for the United States to take a new and hard look at China policy to determine what course of action is desirable both to solve the short-run problem of normalizing relations with Peking and to lay the basis for a viable, lasting U.S.-China relationship and a more stable regional equilibrium in East Asia.

II

A Basis for Future U.S. Policy

THE POLICIES that the United States pursues toward China in the immediate future must be based on a defensible set of general premises and aims. The first premise should be that it is necessary, desirable, and feasible to expand and improve U.S.-China relations in the years immediately ahead, and that this should be a major goal of overall U.S. foreign policy. This may appear self-evident; yet even some Americans who approve the current limited détente question whether further compromises with Peking are now in the U.S. interest. Without efforts at further improvement, however, the present limited relationship could deteriorate rather than stabilizing, and if this occurs it may be impossible to deal effectively with the Chinese on a wide range of problems vital to the future of East Asia.

A second premise must be that further improvement of Sino-American relations will not be easy. The process will, at best, be gradual and the obstacles formidable. Further strengthening of ties is by no means certain; it will depend on the priority both Washington and Peking give to the necessity for compromise and mutual accommodation.

Although Sino-American détente has served the interests of both countries, the benefits have by no means been identical. From the U.S. perspective, the greatest gains have been the end of direct U.S.-China confrontation throughout East Asia, which has substantially reduced the dangers of military conflict, and the imposition of new constraints on the Soviet Union, which contribute to the global balance restraining it. Today, the United States has far less reason for concern than in the past about the potential dangers of coordinated, hostile, Communist actions threatening to U.S. interests, especially in East Asia. In addition, it has gained a certain leverage in dealing with both Peking and Moscow, and a degree of tolerance on China's part for many U.S. activities elsewhere in the region.

For the Chinese the gains have been even greater, and of more fundamental significance. From Peking's perspective, the opening to the United States has reduced the dangers of Soviet military attacks or pressures and helped to balance Moscow's power and influence and to check its efforts to work against Chinese interests elsewhere in the region, thereby contributing significantly to China's security. It has also led to greater U.S. tolerance for many of Peking's efforts to expand its political and economic activities, both regionally and globally.

Although both the United States and China have had to make compromises in order to establish even a limited relationship, the gains for both have so far unquestionably outweighed the political costs, even though the impact of U.S.-China détente on other areas in East Asia has set in motion forces for regional change, the consequences of which neither Washington nor Peking can clearly foresee. However, further improvement of their relations will require additional compromises involving greater political problems for both. Nevertheless, the potential benefits are substantially greater than any realized so far, and therefore short-term problems should not be allowed to obscure the possible long-term gains.

The limits of Sino-American détente must also be accepted. One can hope that in the very long run a greatly improved Sino-American relationship might be achieved, leading to close cooperation between the two governments and a broad, friendly interaction between the two societies. This is unlikely in the foreseeable future, however. The ideological gap, conflict of political values, and divergence of many broad foreign policy goals, as well as basic cultural, social, and economic differences between the two countries, are too great. In practical terms, U.S. policy toward China must now be based on a careful assessment of where U.S. and Chinese interests converge and where they conflict.

The Need for Realism

United States policy must be based, first of all, on a realistic definition of American interests and priorities in relation to China and the East Asian region as a whole. To be effective, however, it must take into account basic Chinese attitudes and aspirations. Mutual misperceptions were a major factor contributing to Sino-American confrontation in the past and could easily lead to new misunderstandings and conflicts in the future. Greater understanding will not eliminate conflicts of values and interests. Expectations therefore should not be unrealistic; if they are, they will lead to new frustrations and disappointments.

No U.S. policy can be successful unless it takes into account the deep-rooted security concerns underlying recent and current Chinese policies toward all the major powers in East Asia. Washington must recognize that China's relative military weakness makes its leaders extremely sensitive to external pressures or threats. The United States should try, therefore, to minimize the basis for Chinese fears, avoiding threats itself and making clear that it opposes threats against China by any other major power. It should be a premise of U.S. policy that the achievement of a greater sense of security on China's part is likely to enhance rather than harm the prospects for peace and stability in East Asia.

The United States must also understand the Chinese leaders' desire to be fully accepted as a major power and to assume larger international roles, both regionally and globally. But American responses to particular Chinese policies should be carefully discriminating: any effort generally to oppose the expansion of Chinese influence abroad would be unjustified; yet American policymakers should make clear that they will continue to oppose policies that could raise tensions, threaten stability, or run counter to broad American international goals. Washington can view with equanimity Chinese policies aimed at achieving legitimate national objectives through peaceful means, and it should encourage China's constructive involvement in the international community. However, it should not attempt to disguise or gloss over conflicts of interest.

A number of conflicts of interest will continue to make U.S.-China relations extremely complex. The two countries' interests in Taiwan will continue to diverge, and no final resolution of the Taiwan problem is likely for many years. More broadly, even though the two countries now share certain important common security interests which are the fundamental basis for their present relationship, American and Chinese outlooks continue to differ in basic respects even in security terms. Both desire to avoid bilateral military conflict, and to limit the expansion of Soviet power and influence, but the current Chinese aim appears to be to manipulate the balance of power for broadly anti-Soviet purposes, while the U.S. aim is to reduce tensions and achieve greater stability in relationships among all the major powers in East Asia.

China's continued encouragement of revolutionary change abroad and its activist role as a would-be Third World leader in exerting political and economic pressures on the developed nations conflict with U.S. interests and policies in many areas and on many issues. In contrast to China's objectives, the U.S. aim is to promote evolutionary change in the context of an international environment that contributes to reduced tensions, minimizes violence, and promotes both equity and stability. It is reasonable at present for the United States to assume that China will continue to pursue its major goals primarily through prudent, low-risk policies, relying essentially on political rather than military means. Nevertheless, the United States cannot ignore the possibility of renewed conflict any more than Peking can or will.

In sum, U.S. policy must be based on the premise that further progress in Sino-American détente is possible, and important to strive for, but that the two countries will continue to be competitors in many respects. Even under the most favorable circumstances, China and the United States will often be adversaries. Accepting this, the American aim should be to reduce, step by step, the areas of tension and conflict, and to gradually broaden the areas of mutual accommodation, recognizing that there is no formula for rapidly resolving all differences or radically transforming Sino-American relations.

The minimum immediate objective of U.S. policy toward China must be to consolidate present relationships, institutionalize them, and reduce the risk that a reversal of Chinese policy might occur, leading to a deterioration of relations once again. The possibility of a reversal cannot be excluded, since Chinese policy could shift if Sino-Soviet relations improve and this reduces Peking's fears of a Soviet threat, or if further leadership changes in China bring to power men inclined toward a more militant policy, or, perhaps as a result of internal political pressures, if Chinese leaders decide to push harder to achieve control of Taiwan. To minimize the possibility of a deterioration, further steps are required to consolidate relations.

The long-term U.S. aim, clearly, should be to go further: to develop gradually a variety of interlocking interests that will create a more solid basis than exists at present for a stable, long-lasting relationship. Even though Peking may view the relationship, in Maoist terms, as "limited" and "temporary," these concepts are inherently elastic, and future Chinese policies will be determined primarily by the leaders' assessments of concrete Chinese interests, rather than by abstract concepts or slogans. The

United States must try to ensure that both countries continue to see a
common interest in broadening and strengthening their relationships.

Normalization and the Taiwan Issue

Since 1972 both Washington and Peking have constantly reiterated
their continuing commitment to the Shanghai communiqué.[1] This remarkable document, skillfully drafted, provided the basic framework for
the U.S.-China opening. After stating explicitly the many fundamental
differences between the two countries, it identified certain important
common interests and goals and defined the basis of a new relationship
involving limited compromise by both sides, without requiring either
side to abandon its most important positions and principles. It implied a
mutual willingness to lay aside or postpone certain critical issues. It also
required deliberate ambiguity, which made compromise, and the start of
a new relationship, possible, but which inevitably involved risks of differing interpretations and new misunderstandings and frictions in the future.

The communiqué started with sections in which both sides stated,
"candidly," their differing policies not only on broad international issues
but also toward many specific areas, including Vietnam, Southeast Asia,
and South Asia. Both sides then declared, however, that they wished to
make "progress toward the normalization of relations" and "to reduce
the danger of international military conflict." They pledged that neither
would "seek hegemony in the Asia-Pacific Region" and they declared
that both would oppose efforts by any other country or group of countries to do so—a clear reference to their common interest in opposing
possible Soviet threats.

The most difficult issue that had to be dealt with was the "crucial question" of Taiwan, the cause of the "long-standing serious dispute" which
for more than twenty years had been the most important single issue
blocking U.S.-China ties. Peking reaffirmed its basic position that "the
Government of the People's Republic of China is the sole legal government of China," that "Taiwan is a province of China which has long been
returned to the motherland," and that "the liberation of Taiwan is
China's internal affair." It also asserted that "all U.S. forces and military
installations must be withdrawn from Taiwan." However, there was no
direct reference in the document to Washington's diplomatic relations

1. See *Department of State Bulletin*, Mar. 20, 1972, pp. 435–38.

and defense treaty with Taiwan, despite Peking's view that full normalization of U.S.-China relations required the end of both. Peking's major concession, actually, was its willingness to begin steps toward normalizing relations before the Taiwan question had been resolved, which for many years it had said it would not do.

In the communiqué, although the United States did not accept Peking's sweeping claims, it did "acknowledge" that "all Chinese on either side of the Taiwan Strait maintain that there is but one China and that Taiwan is a part of China," and it stated that "the United States Government does not challenge that position." It also said that it "reaffirms its interest in a peaceful settlement of the Taiwan issue by the Chinese themselves," adding that "with this prospect in mind" it would "progressively reduce its forces and military installations on Taiwan as the tension in the area diminishes," without giving any definite timetable.

Although the two countries stressed their desire to make "progress toward the normalization of relations," the communiqué did not specify what the prerequisites of full normalization would be or what kind of future compromise on the Taiwan issue might make it possible. However, the establishment of full diplomatic relations between Peking and Tokyo shortly thereafter, and Chinese statements since that time, have somewhat clarified the extent and limits of the compromises that Peking is willing to make. Despite important differences in the problems entailed in normalization for Japan and for the United States, the so-called Japanese model for dealing with the issues is clearly relevant to the United States.

In the Japanese case, Peking insisted that Tokyo sever formal diplomatic relations with the Nationalists, but Tokyo made clear that it would continue de facto political and economic ties with Taiwan, and Peking acquiesced to this. And although Japan recognized the People's Republic as the "sole legal government" of China, it did not explicitly recognize, as Peking had previously insisted, that Taiwan already is a part of China; instead it reiterated its support of the postwar Potsdam declaration and Cairo agreement that Taiwan "should be returned" to China.

Subsequently, Peking has made fairly clear certain of its prerequisites, in regard to Taiwan, for full normalization of its relations with the United States. It insists that the United States must: (1) sever formal diplomatic relations with the Nationalist regime; (2) end the existing U.S. security treaty with it; and (3) withdraw all U.S. military forces and installations from Taiwan. It has indicated, however, that the Japanese model can be the starting point for working out a basis for full diplomatic relations, thus implying that it is prepared to accept continuing de facto U.S. political and economic relations with Taiwan.

This by no means answers all the complex questions that must be dealt with if Washington and Peking try seriously to complete "the process of normalization." Specific mutual compromises on the key issues can only be reached through further negotiations. The United States must first decide what positions it should adopt regarding the Taiwan problem. The basis of further compromise, and the limits of compromise from Washington's point of view, must be spelled out.

Clearly the United States must now accept the necessity of altering its relations with Taiwan in order to upgrade and consolidate its ties with Peking.[2] It should do so, however, only if there is evidence that Peking is also willing to make further compromises and that full normalization of relations will at least open the door to discussion of a wide range of issues affecting peace and stability in East Asia. The kind of immediate changes the United States is prepared to accept must be compatible with a long-term U.S. policy toward Taiwan.

In regard to diplomatic relations, some Americans propose simply downgrading diplomatic ties with Taiwan (for example, maintaining either liaison missions, such as now exist in Peking and Washington, or consular missions). In theory this would be desirable, but it is very likely that Peking will refuse, as it has for the past quarter century. The form of other nations' ties to Taiwan has great symbolic importance to Peking because it claims the island as Chinese territory. The United States must, therefore, be prepared to consider changing the form while continuing much of the substance of its relations with Taiwan. It could do this by following the Japanese precedent and downgrading its political ties with Taiwan to "nonofficial" status.[3] If it does, it should make sure that Peking fully understands and accepts the fact that the United States intends, for the foreseeable future, to maintain de facto political as well as economic, cultural, and other links to Taiwan.

2. My views on certain of the key issues have changed as international circumstances have changed; for my past positions, see *Communist China and Asia: Challenge to American Policy* (Harper, 1960), especially pp. 384 ff.; statement, in *U.S. Policy with Respect to Mainland China*, Hearings before the Senate Foreign Relations Committee, 89:2 (Government Printing Office, 1966), pp. 3–16; and *A New U.S. Policy Toward China* (Brookings Institution, 1971).

3. Secretary of State Kissinger stated in Peking at the end of President Ford's December 1975 visit to China that "the Chinese have made clear that the general model that they want is something similar to the Japanese model" (*Department of State Bulletin*, Dec. 29, 1975, p. 929).

While the United States can look to the Japanese precedent as a model for adjusting diplomatic ties, in other aspects the problem facing Washington is fundamentally different. For more than two decades the United States has been firmly committed by treaty to the defense of Taiwan, and from Washington's perspective the security of Taiwan remains a key issue. Peking insists that the United States must end its mutual security treaty with Taipei, and it is widely accepted among specialists in the U.S. government that the treaty would automatically lapse if Washington severs formal diplomatic relations with the Nationalists. However, under existing circumstances the United States cannot consider a total abandonment of U.S. interest in the Taiwan area or of responsibility for the security of the island. A total disengagement would be regarded by the people on Taiwan and many elsewhere as a betrayal, and it could have very destabilizing effects regionally, in ways that would clearly be adverse to U.S. interests. It might stimulate desperation moves by Taiwan —for example, steps to assert its immediate de jure independence, or to try to form links with Moscow, or to develop an independent nuclear capability—which would greatly complicate the problems of achieving regional stability.

The United States should indicate to Peking, therefore, that it will end the formal defense treaty with Taiwan only if some kind of substitute for it can be devised. What would be desirable, obviously, from the U.S. point of view, would be a firm commitment from Peking that it renounces the use of force in regard to Taiwan, but it may be unrealistic to hope for a commitment that Peking has for two decades adamantly refused to make on the grounds that it would compromise Chinese claims that the Taiwan problem is a domestic issue. The United States can insist that Peking restate that its intention is to strive for reunification of Taiwan by peaceful rather than military means. However, since any such statement is likely to be hedged, and would in no way be binding, its value will be limited. The position that the United States itself asserts will be more important. Washington should, therefore, make a strong, unilateral, public statement of the premises that will underlie its own future policy concerning Taiwan, formulated in such a way that it will create a substitute of sorts for its past defense commitment, and it should obtain at least tacit acquiescence from Peking to such a statement. The United States should state that American policy will be based on the belief that preservation of peace and security in the Taiwan area is important to stability in East Asia, and therefore to U.S. interests, and it should make clear that the United States will continue to oppose any attempt to change Taiwan's status by force. It should indicate—implicitly if necessary to make it possible for Peking to acquiesce to such a statement—that if there is a new threat of military conflict involving Taiwan, the United States will be compelled to reassess its policy toward the area and will consider whatever action appears necessary to try to deter such a conflict or to help defend Taiwan. Without any formal treaty commitment to Taiwan, there would obviously be no automatic use of American military forces if such a contingency were to arise, but the U.S. government should nevertheless indicate that employment of American naval and air power would be possible in the event of conflict.

A position such as this would obviously be a poor substitute for a formal defense treaty if a military attack on Taiwan were likely in the near future. However, the danger of attack is low in the period ahead. Peking's present lack of strong amphibious capabilities, Taiwan's substantial military strength and the hundred miles of water protecting it, all minimize the danger; so too do the political and military constraints deriving from the present big-power balance in East Asia. Peking's leaders cannot ignore the probability that any attack against the island would almost certainly have seriously adverse effects on relations with both the United States and Japan, and possibly the Soviet Union. Nor can they overlook the possibility that new military threats could impel Taiwan itself to consider desperation moves.

All of these factors will tend to deter military conflict in the area even in the absence of any U.S.-Taiwan defense treaty. The need for a statement of the continuing American concern about, and sense of responsibility for, preservation of peace in the Taiwan area is as much political as military, therefore. The purpose of such a statement would be to reduce Taiwan's anxieties, to reassure other concerned nations in East Asia that the United States is not abandoning its regional security responsibilities, and to reinforce Peking's present restraint.

The United States should be prepared to remove all U.S. military forces and installations from Taiwan. But it should make clear that it will allow sales—direct or indirect—of military equipment to the Taipei regime to continue. If it did not do this, Taiwan might very well consider desperation moves which neither Washington nor Peking desires. Washington should strictly limit the amounts and types of military equipment sold to Taiwan, however, restricting sales to materiel essential for the defense of the island, and in any direct supply of materiel it should move toward cash sales rather than sales financed by U.S. government credit.

Continuing military sales may be the most difficult issue on which Chinese acquiescence is required in the next stage of compromise between Washington and Peking. It may be desirable to finesse the issue, formally speaking, rather than confronting it head-on, even though this would increase the risks of friction at a later date. But so long as Peking is unwilling to renounce the use of force against Taiwan, the United States should not agree to end all military help to Taiwan, since doing so could undermine Taiwan's capacity to defend itself.

While adopting the policy positions suggested above, the United States should also clarify its views on Taiwan's political future. Washington should reemphasize that the United States will not oppose future changes in Taiwan's status, either toward reunification with China or ultimate autonomy, if such changes can be worked out peacefully by the Chinese themselves, including those both on Taiwan and in China. More positively, the United States should make it clear that it would view with approval the establishment of contacts leading to exploration of the possibilities for an eventual political modus vivendi between Peking and Taipei. But the United States should not itself assume responsibility for trying to solve the Taiwan problem. It should avoid, as it in effect pledged to do in the Shanghai communiqué, challenging Peking's claim that Taiwan is legally a part of China. However, it should also avoid committing itself to the position that Taiwan is already a part of China, not only because the island clearly is not under Peking's control, but also because continuation of even de facto relations with Taiwan could be challenged if the United States were to accept, under existing circumstances, that Taiwan is already a part of China, legally.

At the same time Washington should emphasize, to Taipei as well as to Peking, that under existing circumstances it will not itself support any moves toward de jure independence by Taiwan, which would create complex new problems, at least in the immediate future, that might destabilize relationships in the region. It should also oppose any steps by Taiwan to establish links with the Soviet Union or to work toward acquisition of a nuclear capability. However, it should not try itself to determine what the future status of Taiwan should be, except to maintain its position that it is prepared to accept any solution arrived at peacefully by the Chinese themselves.

The course of action suggested above will only be feasible, obviously, if both Washington and Peking are prepared to make significant new compromises. While from the American point of view the severance of diplomatic ties with Taiwan and the ending of the existing security treaty with the Nationalists will appear to involve the greatest concessions, Peking's leaders will feel that the acceptance by them, even tacitly, of the continuation of informal U.S. military as well as political and economic ties with Taiwan involves major compromises on their part. They may fear the result could be an indefinite perpetuation of the status quo, or even eventual Taiwanese independence. Although the United States cannot assure Peking that this will not be the result, it can indicate that while continuing to maintain a friendly informal relationship with Taiwan, it will reduce its involvement in the island's domestic affairs and gradually modify and loosen the kind of political ties that have existed between the United States and Taiwan in the past. Steps in this direction should be very gradual, however, and they should be contingent on the continued absence of military threats to Taiwan and calibrated to parallel progress in the improvement of overall U.S.-China relations, the establishment eventually of some kind of dialogue between China and Taiwan, and the stabilization of conditions in the region generally.

The U.S. policy suggested here obviously will not solve the Taiwan problem. There simply is no formula for its immediate solution. It will, moreover, create new ambiguities which may be difficult for Washington to cope with. Yet it is preferable to other options. Standing pat could risk a deterioration, or even a reversal, of U.S.-China relations, and total disengagement from any responsibility for the fate of Taiwan and its sixteen million people could have seriously adverse effects on U.S. interests throughout the region.

The government and people on Taiwan will undoubtedly feel that in pursuing such a policy the United States is sacrificing many of their interests. Taiwan will not find it easy to accept being in an even greater diplomatic limbo than at present. Yet the continuation of U.S. efforts to deter any military attack on Taiwan and to ensure the island's economic viability and survival in a de facto sense will represent a significant commitment on the U.S. part. In the immediate future, at least, this is the best Taiwan can hope for. The kind of two-Chinas solution to the Taiwan problem that might have been a realistic possibility in the 1950s and 1960s, is not a realistic option at present. No matter how tempting some kind of independent de jure status may appear, Taiwan's leaders cannot ignore the reality that in the years immediately ahead moves in that direction would probably damage its economic and other nonofficial ties throughout the world, thereby increasing its isolation.

It is likely that Peking will accept continued economic and nonofficial political relations between Washington and Taipei, since it has done essentially that in the case of Japan. But there is no certainty that it will acquiesce to any kind of substitute for the U.S.-Taiwan security treaty and to continued sales of military materiel to Taiwan. If it does not, the present minimal U.S.-China relationship seems likely to continue, with unavoidable risks of a reversal or deterioration. The seeming willingness of many Chinese Communist leaders to view the Taiwan problem in long-range terms gives a basis for hoping, however, that understandings can be reached. There are strong arguments in favor of the United States taking the steps it must as soon as possible, because of the uncertainties that changes of leadership in China have introduced.

Even if the United States and China can compromise on the Taiwan issue sufficiently to make normalization of U.S.-China relations possible, the problem will not have been solved. Unavoidable ambiguities will continue, and these could cause new tensions in the future. The Chinese will still stress the need for further change, while the United States will continue to emphasize the need for stability, and this basic difference is not likely to disappear.

Washington will immediately face numerous problems in adjusting its laws and policies to deal with the new situation, and Peking may strongly object to some of the steps required. Numerous laws and regulations will have to be revised,[4] for example, to facilitate continued normal intercourse between the United States and Taiwan, since the regime there will no longer be legally viewed in the United States as the government of a recognized state but rather as a de facto regime on a territory whose legal status remains ambiguous. It would be remarkable if the new U.S. legislation and revisions of administrative regulations required did not include wording, or were not accompanied by debates or

4. In early 1976, 55 agreements were in force between the governments of the United States and the Republic of China on Taiwan. Presumably the U.S. government has already started detailed analysis of how existing laws and regulations would have to be modified and what new ones would be required if Taiwan were no longer officially recognized by the United States. One way of dealing with the problem would be for the U.S. Congress to include many of the required legal actions in an omnibus bill passed at the time that formal U.S. recognition is transferred from Taipei to Peking.

statements, that aroused Peking's ire. Even the basic question of how Taiwan and its government are to be referred to in legal documents may not be easily resolved without evoking protests from Peking or Taipei or both. The problems of conducting governmental relations with Taiwan through nonofficial channels will tax the ingenuity and flexibility of U.S. bureaucrats and legal specialists. Japan's solution has been to set up a nonofficial diplomatic mission in Taiwan that consists of men who have temporarily resigned from the diplomatic service, yet are paid by it, indirectly, and report to it. It remains to be seen how well the U.S. government will be able to cope with such problems, in what will be a highly unorthodox relationship.

In implementing the policy outlined above, moreover, it will be essential to continue, and perhaps in the immediate future even to expand, U.S. economic and cultural relationships with Taiwan, to help ensure the island's economic viability and morale. The psychological impact of changes in Taiwan's legal status on businessmen in the United States and elsewhere is uncertain. Traders may not be greatly disturbed by the change, but investors could have new doubts about Taiwan's future. Special efforts will probably be required to encourage U.S. investments, through continuing investment guarantees, another matter that will probably require new legislation. There are good reasons nevertheless for confidence that Taiwan will continue to be a viable economic entity. The recent economic development of the island is remarkable: during the 1960s its gross national product grew at a rate of roughly 10 percent a year, and although growth was set back by the worldwide oil crisis and depression in the early 1970s, the basic resiliency and adaptability of Taiwan's economy has been demonstrated by its subsequent recovery.

In a broad sense it is not easy to predict the political impact of all these developments on Taiwan. It seems probable that its leaders will adjust realistically to the new situation. Yet it is possible that confidence in the future could weaken, with unpredictable political as well as economic effects. The United States should do what it can to minimize this possibility.

There will probably be problems in convincing the American Congress and public that even though the United States no longer officially recognizes the regime on Taiwan, it nevertheless has continuing responsibilities toward it, which require economic and other measures to help ensure its viability. In the present mood in the United States, questions concerned with military security will be especially difficult to deal with.

The United States must decide whether simply to ignore the Nationalists' policy of stationing large numbers of troops on the offshore islands, where several military crises have occurred in the past, or to make clear to Taipei that the United States excludes these islands from the area to which its Taiwan policies apply, and to pressure the Nationalists to withdraw all, or most, of their forces there. Even though past U.S. attempts to convince the Nationalists not to station large numbers of troops on these islands have failed, the effort should continue. These troops may not pose immediate problems, but they perpetuate a situation that could become a focus for crisis and conflict in the future. If Peking's policy were to shift back to one of military pressure on Taiwan, it could again precipitate a crisis, with minimum immediate risk to itself, simply by ordering a massive artillery barrage, or it could try to blockade the islands and might succeed, if there were no U.S. intervention. Taiwan may continue to resist the idea of withdrawing its troops, because of the offshore islands' symbolism as a link to the mainland, but Washington should continue to urge Taipei's withdrawal. It should make clear that the United States will avoid involvement in a new local crisis. It should also consider restricting the use of American arms sold to Taiwan to the defense of Taiwan itself and the Pescadores.

Another difficult question for the United States is whether American oil companies should be permitted to operate in the ocean areas surrounding Taiwan where Peking as well as Taipei claims ownership of the oil, and where the Communists could easily create incidents if they chose to do so.[5] Recently, the U.S. government has discouraged American drilling in disputed areas and has encouraged companies operating in the area to use foreign crews and rigs. It has also told at least one American oil company that it would not be advisable to drill more than two hundred miles from Taiwan. However, many ambiguities remain; if an attempt is made, for example, to restrict the operation of U.S. companies to clearly demarcated areas, Peking might choose to interpret such a move as an attempt to define, and limit, its areas of jurisdiction. Nevertheless, the U.S. government should informally designate boundaries beyond which American companies should not drill, to minimize the risk

5. See Selig S. Harrison, "China: The Next Oil Giant," *Foreign Policy*, no. 20 (Fall 1975), especially pp. 9 ff.

of incidents involving Peking, at the same time making clear that it will accept whatever jurisdictional boundaries in the area are agreed upon in the future by the authorities most directly involved.

Still another complex issue centers on whether the United States should assist Taiwan in developing military industries that would enhance its independent defense capabilities. Since discouragement of such development would virtually ensure Taiwan's continued dependence on certain types of U.S. military equipment, the question poses difficult dilemmas. Already Washington has assisted in the development of certain new military industries on Taiwan. For example, in 1973 it authorized a credit worth about $250 million under which the Northrop Corporation has licensed production of F-5E fighter aircraft on Taiwan.[6] There is clearly a logic to doing this, since it enhances Taiwan's ability to ensure its own defense without direct U.S. involvement. Under existing circumstances, it seems justifiable, but if continued it should be highly selective and its scale limited, and the United States should make wholly clear that it is not assisting in a major military buildup or in developing production of weapons that are primarily useful for offensive operations. Whether such assistance should continue after full normalization of Washington-Peking ties is an open question. However, even if the United States ends such assistance, it should be prepared to facilitate sales of defensive military equipment to Taiwan so long as there appears to be a danger of military conflict in the area, and until a peaceful resolution of Taiwan's future status appears possible.

All of these issues could create difficult problems for the United States in its relations with both Peking and Taipei. There is a good possibility also that even if Peking acquiesces to sales of military equipment to Taiwan in the immediate future, it might choose to make it an issue of contention later.

The greatest uncertainty concerns Peking's future overall policy toward Taiwan. Even if Peking does not attempt to mount a military invasion of the island, it may decide at some point to exert pressures of a more subtle sort that could endanger Taiwan's economic viability and weaken its morale. It might, for example, try to induce businessmen in Japan, or Europe, or even the United States, to cut back or halt their trade and investments in Taiwan, perhaps by open threats to discriminate

6. See Joseph Lelyveld, "A 1½ China Policy," *New York Times Magazine*, April 6, 1975; and Senator Mike Mansfield, *China: A Quarter Century After the Founding of the People's Republic* (Government Printing Office, 1975), p. 22.

against them in China trade, or by more indirect means. A concerted effort to erode Taiwan's economic and other nonofficial ties abroad would have disquieting effects.

The initiation at some point of a dialogue, and economic contacts, between Taipei and Peking, must be hoped for, since the Taiwan problem will continue to pose a latent threat to peace and stability in the region until some sort of modus vivendi is reached between China and Taiwan. This may take years—even decades—and until it occurs, the Taiwan problem will not only not be solved, it will only have been partially shelved.

If a prolonged period of time passes without progress toward a modus vivendi between China and Taiwan, political pressures are likely to operate in the direction of Taiwanese independence. Although there now appears to be little prospect that Peking's leaders could accept and accommodate peacefully to such a development, conceivably at some point in the future they might be able to do so. However, they remain bitterly hostile to the idea today, and if Taiwan were to declare independence before some kind of understanding with Peking is achieved, this could pose in stark terms the dilemma of whether the United States should give priority to its relations with China or to the assertion by the sixteen million people on Taiwan of the right of self-determination. Today the issue is not one of self-determination in its classic form, since the governments in both Peking and Taipei still assert the principle of Chinese unity, even though the majority of people on Taiwan oppose reunification under existing conditions. But it could become such an issue in the future. If so, the United States would then have to reexamine its policies and make new decisions in the context of the total situation at that time.[7]

7. Taiwan's present situation, attitudes, and interests, and its possible long-run future, are discussed in greater detail in a companion volume, *China and the Major Powers in East Asia* (Brookings, 1977).

III

A New Agenda of Issues

ALTHOUGH the establishment of formal diplomatic ties with Peking is required to remove a fundamental barrier to significant forward movement in the U.S.-China relationship, or at least to prevent it from deteriorating, this symbolic step will not automatically produce immediate major changes in the substance of relationships. It will simply open the door to further efforts to deal with important problems. The difficult task of institutionalizing and expanding ties will still lie ahead.

From the U.S. point of view, the list of problems that must be on the agenda is a long one. Some involve essentially bilateral issues. Others involve complex multilateral relationships.

The problems that can be dealt with first are those relating to bilateral trade and other economic relationships, and to the development of scientific, technical, and cultural exchanges. Although these are not the most important issues in U.S.-China relations, they could be significant in the long run, and they probably can be dealt with relatively soon. Far more important, because they concern fundamental issues of war or peace, are problems relating to military security and arms control. These involve much more complex, sensitive, and difficult questions which will at best take considerable time to deal with. All of these bilateral issues are analyzed in this chapter.

United States policy toward China must also be examined in the context of multilateral relationships. In defining its China policy, the United States cannot ignore the side effects on other nations; conversely, in formulating other policies it must consider the implications for U.S.-China relations. It is necessary, therefore, to examine China policy in relation to the emerging four-power equilibrium in East Asia, the tri-

34

angular relationships among the United States, the Soviet Union, and China, and the United States, Japan, and China, the interactions of the major powers in Korea and Southeast Asia, and the global relationships between the developed and developing nations. These are discussed in chapter 4.

In each of these problem areas, the United States must, after identifying the key issues, decide what is desirable from the point of view of American interests, try to determine what is feasible, and define its policies accordingly. It will not be possible to address all of the problems at once; difficult choices will have to be made. Moreover, Peking's list of what should be on the agenda will differ from Washington's. The Chinese can be expected to resist even discussing some of the issues that Americans consider important. On the issues that are joined, they will doubtless try to drive hard bargains. The process of interaction is certain to be difficult and at times frustrating, therefore. Nevertheless, the United States must commit itself to a continuing search for means to reduce differences and conflicts of interest, to minimize tensions and frictions, to broaden areas of tacit agreement or parallelism in policy, to promote gradual steps toward mutual accommodation, and to create over time the basis for expanded Sino-American cooperation.

Economic Relations

The rapid rise of U.S.-China trade, from $5 million in 1971 to $934 million in 1974, was one of the most dramatic and visible symbols of the improvement of Sino-American relations. However, the fairly precipitous drop in the trade in 1975, to $495 million,[1] highlighted the fact that economic relations between the two countries are still tenuous. Much needs to be done to create a more stable foundation for trade over the long term. In approaching this problem, a realistic view must be taken of both the opportunities and the obstacles to further expansion of U.S.-

1. Central Intelligence Agency, *People's Republic of China: International Trade Handbook*, research aid A(ER) 75-73 (CIA, 1975), p. 9, and "China: Trade, By Area and Country, 1974–1975" (CIA, May 1976; processed). For background on U.S.-China trade, see Alexander Eckstein, "China's Trade Policy and Sino-American Relations," *Foreign Affairs*, vol. 54 (October 1975), pp. 134–54, and "China's Economic Growth and Foreign Trade," *U.S.-China Business Review*, July–August 1974, pp. 15–20; and Nai-Ruenn Chen, "China's Trade, 1950–74," in Joint Economic Committee, *China: A Reassessment of the Economy* (GPO, 1975).

China economic relations. The potential significance of economic relationships also needs to be weighted in terms of long-run as well as short-run goals and assessed in terms of U.S. political as well as economic interests.

From a short-term and strictly economic perspective, economic ties with China are of minor importance in relation to overall U.S. economic interests. Even under the most optimistic assumptions, trade with China is not likely to exceed one or two percent of total U.S. trade in the years immediately ahead. There is no foreseeable prospect for any direct U.S. investment in China, and at best only limited forms of licensing and other arrangements for technical cooperation are likely to develop. Nor is China likely to be a significant supplier of commodities that are critical to the U.S. economy. Americans can obviously benefit from access to certain Chinese resources, such as nonferrous minerals, and if China should be willing and able to export oil in significant quantities to the United States as well as to Japan (which seems unlikely soon) this would clearly be in the U.S. interest. In the near future, however, it is probable that such trade will not be large enough to be of more than marginal importance in terms of U.S. resource needs.

The potential importance of Sino-American economic relations to China is greater, essentially for two reasons. The Chinese may, in the future as in the past, find it necessary to import significant quantities of agricultural commodities, including grain, of which the United States is the world's largest exporter. If world shortages were severe, and China's needs acute, access to American supplies could be of critical importance to the Chinese. More important, China will doubtless have a continuing need to obtain sophisticated capital goods and advanced scientific and technological know-how from the principal industrial nations. Even though there are alternative sources of supply in Japan and Western Europe for most of what the Chinese want, Peking could decide to turn increasingly to American sources for certain products and types of knowledge, because the United States is the world's most advanced industrial nation. Though a great many economic and political variables could affect the level of Chinese imports from the United States, the prospect is for some increase, over time, if overall relations continue to improve.

The growth of Sino-American trade will almost certainly be gradual, however. China's capacity to expand its exports to the United States, which is now very limited, will probably increase only slowly, and

Peking is not likely to accept any great imbalance in favor of the United States over an extended period of time. Moreover, future leaders will probably try to avoid excessive economic dependence on any nation, which would impose an upper limit on Sino-American trade even under favorable circumstances.

For all of these reasons, the potential size and the economic importance of China trade to the United States should not be exaggerated. The significance of the political and psychological impact of growing economic ties should not be underestimated, however. Trade relations will be viewed, correctly, as an important measure of the degree to which both countries are serious about their desire to develop their overall relationship. Economic relationships, moreover, constitute an area in which ideological and other political obstacles are relatively easy to deal with. In this area also intersocietal contact, however limited, can gradually grow, and over time help to increase mutual understanding and promote cooperation.

To be sure, economic relationships between socialist societies, which operate through state trading organizations, and pluralistic, capitalistic societies, in which transactions are carried out by private enterprises, inevitably involve difficult problems. Moreover, there is little basis for believing that economic interests will be the primary determinant of Peking's political policies. China has demonstrated on many occasions that when political and economic goals diverge, the former usually take precedence, as was the case in Sino-Soviet relations. Nevertheless, in the long run, the interlocking interests that economic intercourse builds up should help to strengthen political relationships. Washington should place considerable importance, therefore, on the goal of increasing U.S.-China trade, for political as well as economic reasons.

Expanded U.S.-China trade may help China avert serious domestic economic failures that would cause social tensions and political strife. Even though the linkages between internal problems and foreign policy in China as elsewhere are far from clear, the United States should base its future policy on the premise that a stable China that is able to cope with its most pressing economic problems and sees hopeful prospects for continuing its domestic development in a peaceful international environment is more likely to fit into a stable equilibrium in East Asia—or at least less likely to pose serious threats to it—than a turbulent China. This is not a premise that is universally accepted. There are some who believe that anything that weakens an adversary is desirable in terms of U.S. interests. However, the weight of history supports the presumption that major powers that encounter serious economic crises are more likely to pose threats to international stability than those whose prospects for peaceful development are good.

The United States' economic relationships with China thus should be aimed in part at helping China to solve some of its basic domestic problems and to sustain a process of continuing economic growth. In broad terms, U.S. policy should be motivated by a desire to help China develop its agriculture and civilian industries, rather than to damage China economically and slow its growth, as the U.S. embargo of the 1950s and 1960s sought (rather ineffectively) to do. Following the normalization of diplomatic relations with Peking, Washington should adopt flexible and liberal policies regarding both the transfer of technology and the extension of credits to China.

Issues concerning technology transfers are certain to be increasingly important as U.S.-China economic relations expand. Among the difficult questions, indicative of the varied and complex problems that are likely to arise, is one that the United States faced in 1975. China, in its search for new technology, showed an active interest in purchasing advanced types of U.S. computers which would be immensely useful for oil development. Because the computers could also be used to improve China's defense capabilities, the U.S. government debated for more than a year whether to approve the sale; it finally did so in late 1976.[2]

Problems such as these will have to be considered individually, on a case-by-case basis, but as a general policy the United States should look with favor on sales to China of technology that will help its economic growth and should narrow the limits of what is barred because of "strategic" classifications. In view of China's relatively weak military position and its primarily defensive posture, Washington need not be excessively concerned if items sold to China for economic development projects also have some military utility.

Because of the differences that exist today between the Chinese and Soviet societies and economies, decisions on permission to sell particular

2. See *New York Times*, Oct. 4, 1975, and Oct. 29, 1976. For evidence of recent debate in China on the issue of whether to try to obtain foreign militarily relevant technology and equipment, see "Wei Yuan's Thought Against Aggression," from the magazine *Wen-wu*, translated in *Selections from People's Republic of China Magazines*, CMP-SPRCM-75-27, no. 838 (Sept. 15, 1975), especially pp. 4–6.

items to these two countries need not be identical. It would be unwise, however, in the context of the United States' triangular relationship with these countries, to pursue a licensing policy that discriminates blatantly in favor of either China or the Soviet Union. As a general rule the United States should be willing to sell to one items that it is prepared to sell to the other. In many cases, however, the Russians may already possess items roughly equivalent to those the Chinese wish to buy since Soviet technology is considerably more advanced than China's.[3]

The question of whether or not to provide credits to China could also become an important issue. Generally, the Chinese have handled imports from the United States on a pay-as-you-go basis, but they have increasingly sought short- and medium-term credits elsewhere, in Japan and Europe. Because of China's strong commitment to self-reliance, most of these have been in disguised forms ("extended-payment" arrangements being most common), but Peking's inhibitions against accepting foreign credits have weakened as China's need for financing has grown. China had a foreign trade deficit of close to $1 billion in 1974 and over $350 million in 1975, and significant deficits could continue.[4] If so, Peking's desire for foreign credits is likely to grow. There is a good possibility, therefore, that the Chinese will become interested in obtaining U.S. credits, especially if they decide to expand trade with the United States.

On this, as on the issue of technology transfers, the United States should adopt a flexible and liberal policy. To facilitate the further development of U.S.-China trade, it should actively encourage the extension of both short- and medium-term credits on reasonable terms. The possibilities in this respect will be limited, however, until trade legislation is changed to allow the U.S. Export-Import Bank to provide credits, and guarantees for credits extended by private American sources, to China as well as the Soviet Union. This may be some time off. In the meantime the U.S. government should at least look favorably on private credit arrangements made with the Chinese. (The Chinese record in repaying loans and credits has been excellent.)

Credits offered to Peking should certainly be on no less favorable terms than those offered to Moscow. In the case of neither country,

3. In some instances, however, the Russians' willingness, and Chinese unwillingness, to state clearly the end use of items desired may mean that Peking cannot buy what the Russians can.
4. CIA, *People's Republic of China*, and "China: Trade."

however, would it be justifiable for the United States to adopt credit policies more favorable than those applied to the principal noncommunist developing nations. The availability of credits is far from unlimited, and generally priority should be given to the needs of countries whose economic and political values are most compatible with those of the United States. Nevertheless, a generally liberal credit policy toward China is both justifiable and desirable in conjunction with a U.S. policy to expand trade with China and help China solve its basic economic development problems.

The extent to which trade can be expanded will depend less on the credit available, however, than on the degree to which economic relationships can be institutionalized. A series of fairly mundane but important agreements is required to place trade between the two countries on a more regularized and stable basis than at present.[5] During the period following the opening of economic contacts in 1971, U.S.-China economic relations were relatively simple, since most trade resulted from a few large sales of U.S. agricultural commodities to China. In the future, however, if trade expands significantly, it must involve a more equal, two-way exchange of a much wider variety of commodities and goods. To facilitate this, economic agreements of many sorts, both official and nonofficial, will be necessary to institutionalize relationships.

The Chinese position now seems to be that negotiation on most of the issues involved should wait until political ties with the United States are fully normalized, but the United States should be prepared to deal with these issues as soon as Peking is willing. One of the first agreements should be one to settle the assets and claims questions. Although the two countries appeared close to agreement on this in 1973, the Chinese have subsequently dragged their feet. The United States should continue to urge a final settlement of this question as soon as possible. Thereafter, an attempt should be made to negotiate, step by step, a variety of other official bilateral agreements, including, for example, maritime and aviation agreements comparable to those the Japanese have recently signed. Some of these could involve difficult problems, as the Japanese experience in negotiating an aviation agreement indicated, especially if Peking chooses

5. The kinds of agreements needed are discussed in Jerome Alan Cohen, "Implications of Détente for Sino-American Trade," in Gene T. Hsiao, ed., *Sino-American Détente and Its Policy Implications* (Praeger, 1974), pp. 46–75; and in Christopher H. Phillips, *The Present Status of Trade Relations Between the U.S. and the People's Republic of China* (Washington: National Council for U.S.-China Trade, 1975).

to inject political issues concerning Taiwan into such negotiations with the United States.

In time, agreements need to be reached on such diverse matters as patents, trademarks, and copyrights, arbitration procedures, banking arrangements, commodity inspection procedures, treatment of foreign businessmen in China, and so on. Politics is less likely to complicate negotiations on matters of this sort, but reaching agreement may nevertheless be difficult, and take time, simply because of the huge differences that exist between the two societies and economies.

There will be a need also to promote two-way trade through special missions, fairs, and exhibits. Eventually, it may be desirable to establish trade offices or commissions in both countries. It should be U.S. policy to assist the Chinese actively in their efforts to develop and adapt goods for marketing in the United States, since increased U.S. imports from China will be essential if U.S. exports to China are to grow significantly.

The greatest need of all is to grant China most-favored-nation treatment and to negotiate a broad U.S.-China trade agreement. But this will not be easy.[6] Present U.S. law prevents granting most-favored-nation treatment before a general trade agreement has been signed, and the political prerequisites, as well as economic conditions, for a trade agreement will be difficult for the Chinese to accept. Although the major political condition, concerning emigration policy, is aimed at the Soviet Union (specifically at Moscow's treatment of Soviet Jews), it applies to other countries as well, and Peking is even less likely to modify its emigration policy in response to American political pressures than Moscow is. Modification of this legislation is highly desirable, therefore, if the United States seriously wishes to encourage U.S.-China trade. It is not desirable, in my view, to use trade policy as a means of political pressure on emigration policy, in regard to either the Soviet Union or China. If Congress wished to extend most-favored-nation treatment to Peking without all the requirements set in the Trade Act of 1974, it could pass legislation applying to China only. It would be far preferable, however, to modify the trade act itself.

Even if this is done, negotiating a comprehensive trade agreement with China could still be difficult, since Peking's preference, clearly, is to deal with trade issues on a much more ad hoc basis. The United States

6. See Jay F. Henderson, Nicholas H. Ludlow, and Eugene A. Theroux, "China and the Trade Act of 1974," *U.S.-China Business Review*, January–February 1975, pp. 3–10.

should nevertheless hope that eventually such an agreement can be concluded, and it should be as flexible as possible in approaching the problem. If it becomes clear that existing U.S. law makes it impossible to reach a comprehensive trade agreement with China, the feasibility and desirability of modifying existing legislation should be given serious consideration.

To put U.S.-China trade on a more stable and reliable basis, it will be highly desirable, also, to negotiate a long-term agreement on grain trade, comparable to the three-year agreements China has with Canada and Australia. Without such an agreement, the United States will probably remain a residual source of supply for China, and Chinese purchases of American agricultural commodities—and therefore overall U.S.-China trade—could fluctuate tremendously, and unpredictably, as it did during 1972–75.

An agreement concerning Chinese textile exports to the United States may eventually be necessary, if China is successful in its efforts to expand those exports. Though Peking will not find it easy to compete against Taiwan, Hong Kong, Korea, and other nations selling low-cost textiles, if its textile sales to the United States do grow substantially, Washington will doubtless feel compelled to negotiate an agreement similar to others it has limiting textile sales in the United States. Without such an agreement, the United States would in effect be giving preferential treatment to China over its smaller, noncommunist competitors, which would hardly be justifiable even though increased imports from China should in general be welcomed in the United States. If the Chinese are reluctant to accede to U.S. desires in this respect, the textile issue, like many others in the economic field, could create troublesome problems.

The process of institutionalizing U.S.-China economic relations is likely at best to take many years, therefore. Most of the problems involved will not be the kind that make headlines, but they will be a major preoccupation of those in Washington and Peking who are concerned with the day-to-day problems of consolidating the relationship. A large effort will probably have to be made to achieve results that may seem relatively small from a short-term perspective, at least from the U.S. point of view. But to the extent that these efforts succeed, the institutionalization and expansion of trade should gradually build interlocking interests that can contribute significantly to a strengthening of overall U.S.-China relations in the long run.

Cultural Relations

Trade has been one highly visible symbol of the improvement of U.S.-China relations since 1971; two-way exchanges have been another. After more than twenty years of virtually no people-to-people contacts, a variety of scientific, technical, cultural, educational, and journalistic contacts have been initiated. The most important of these, as symbols of the present overall relationship and as a means to build significant long-term links between the two societies, have been the exchanges endorsed by the two governments; in addition a sizable one-way flow of Americans to China has occurred.

Judgments about the scale, nature, and importance of these exchanges vary, depending on the criteria used to evaluate and compare them. Some of the Americans who have been involved in fostering planned exchange relationships have been disappointed with the results so far and frustrated by the problems of trying to make the contacts more meaningful and lasting. But when compared with exchanges between China and Western European nations that have full diplomatic relations with Peking, the U.S.-China exchanges seem to have developed reasonably well. When compared, however, with the exchange relationships that China had with the Soviet Union in the 1950s, or that it now has with Japan—or with the kind that exist between most major noncommunist nations—Sino-American contacts are still extremely limited.

As in the case of trade, there are significant asymmetries in the interests that China and the United States have in exchanges, and in the immediate benefits they derive from them. Today the Chinese enjoy more opportunities to work toward certain of their short-run objectives through exchanges than the Americans do. As in the case of trade, also, although exchanges initially developed more rapidly than expected, there are built-in constraints and difficulties, traceable to differing national priorities and the inherent problems of interaction between open and closed societies, that limit their development. If the contacts are to be expanded on a mutually beneficial, stable, and sustainable basis, an improved framework for long-term exchanges will be necessary.

The United States should make a strong effort to develop the contacts further. Even though the more obvious immediate benefits lie on the Chinese side, the less tangible aspects of scientific and cultural contacts could be very important to American interests and goals over the long run. In pursuing their development, the United States must realistically take account of the problems that the first years of the exchange experience have revealed.

Since 1971 Sino-American exchanges have involved over ten thousand American visits to China and visits by about seven hundred Chinese to the United States.[7] Chinese leaders have had several readily identifiable aims, which have been primary determinants of the nature of the evolving exchange relationship. Broadly speaking, they have viewed exchanges as an important symbol of the new overall Sino-American relationship, as has the U.S. government, but in addition they have had more specific objectives. One has been to send carefully selected groups of Chinese scientists and technical experts to the United States, with the aim of acquiring new scientific and technical knowledge in high-priority fields. Since the establishment, during 1972–73, of working relationships between Peking's semiofficial Scientific and Technical Association and the private American Committee on Scholarly Communication with the People's Republic of China (sponsored by the National Academy of Sciences, American Council of Learned Societies, and Social Science Research Council), the Chinese have sent delegations in such diverse fields as high-energy and solid-state physics, laser science, seismology, computer sciences, petrochemical technology, communications, industrial automation, medicine (including delegations focused on immunology and pharmacology), agriculture, hydrotechnology, plant photosynthesis, insect hormone control, language teaching, and library science.[8]

Under the American auspices of the National Committee on United States-China Relations (often cooperating with other private American groups), the Chinese have sent sports groups, performing arts troupes, and exhibitions. These "spectaculars," designed to have a significant impact on public opinion in the United States, have included a table tennis team, the Shenyang acrobatic troupe, a group of gymnasts, a "martial

7. Statement by Douglas P. Murray, in *United States-China Relations: The Process of Normalization of Relations*, Hearings before a Special Subcommittee on Investigations of the House Committee on International Relations (GPO, 1976), p. 54. This discussion draws heavily on sources from the National Committee on U.S.-China Relations, such as *Notes from the National Committee*, and the Committee on Scholarly Communication with the People's Republic of China, such as *China Exchange Newsletter*.

8. For complete listing, see *China Exchange Newsletter*, vol. 3, no. 5 (November 1975), p. 2.

arts" performing troupe, an archeological exhibition, and a women's basketball team, plus a delegation of journalists which is the only one in this category organized primarily for private discussions rather than public performances or exhibitions. The extensive publicity given these groups has served important Chinese public relations purposes.

A third category of visiting Chinese delegations has been those in the trade field, in which the government-endorsed but privately run National Council on United States-China Trade has played the key role on the U.S. side. These have included a general trade promotion group from the China Council for the Promotion of International Trade and several delegations with specialized interests in fields such as textiles.

Close to two-thirds of the Chinese who visited the United States in the period 1972–75 came through "facilitated" exchanges, as both the U.S. and Chinese governments refer to the visits endorsed and assisted by the two governments (in the Shanghai communiqué the two governments pledged to "facilitate" exchanges). Agreements on such exchanges have been reached through a two-track negotiating process: the U.S. and Chinese governments have discussed the exchanges in general terms, but negotiations on specific exchanges have been conducted directly between the three major private American organizations involved and several semiofficial Chinese organizations that handle such matters.

Only one-third or so of the Chinese visiting the United States have come outside of this framework. A few have made privately arranged scientific visits or have attended scientific conferences, and a handful have made private visits for personal reasons. The majority, however, have made business-related visits. The latter have included at least 130 technicians sent for training connected with trade deals; for example, about 80 have received training from the Boeing Company and about 40 from the Kellogg Company.

The scale and nature of U.S. visits to China have been different in several respects. Among the huge number of Americans who have requested visas to visit China, the motivations have been extremely diverse, and the actual flow of Americans to China has been substantially larger than the flow of Chinese to the United States. Most important, the selection of the overwhelming majority of the Americans going to China has been made by the Chinese alone.

Probably, several tens of thousands of Americans (some guesses put the number in the hundreds of thousands) have applied to visit China. Of the more than ten thousand who have actually gone there, only a small percentage (roughly, five hundred people) have gone under facilitated exchanges. For the rest, the Chinese have decided whom they would invite, or turn down or ignore.

The motives of most Americans desiring to go to China, whether under the facilitated exchanges or on direct invitation from the Chinese, have differed significantly from those of most Chinese visitors. Of the large number of American scientists who have wished to visit China, only those in a few fields such as seismology, agriculture, and certain medical specialties have believed they could gain significant knowledge of professional value. Most have wanted above all to satisfy their curiosity about China. Others have gone to try to draw the Chinese into the global scientific community and to establish contacts that might be important for scientific cooperation in the future. The Chinese motives in inviting particular American scientific groups have varied. They have invited some because of their desire to obtain new knowledge from contacts with them, and others, especially in fields in which the Chinese have made visible progress, to try to impress upon them the image of a "new China."

The strongest interest in exchanges among American scholars has been among academic specialists in the social sciences and humanities, especially specialists on Chinese affairs. Their primary desire has been to observe and study Chinese society, not to learn about what the Chinese have done in various academic disciplines. Peking has been fully aware of the breadth of these interests, but it has been very reluctant, for ideological and political reasons, to invite significant numbers of scholars in these fields under the facilitated exchange programs. The few whom the Chinese have invited, mainly on the persistent urging of the American exchange organizations involved, have frequently been frustrated by the severe limits placed on their opportunities to pursue their intellectual interests fruitfully.

The leading American organizations interested in broad cultural contacts with China have been eager to reciprocate visits by Chinese exhibition groups, performing arts troupes, and sports delegations by sending similar groups to China, but they have placed a much higher priority on sending American public affairs and educational groups to China, in the hope that they might engage some Chinese in serious discussions of major issues of concern to both countries—to try, in short, to initiate a dialogue between key groups in the two societies. The Chinese, under constant prodding, have accepted a few such groups but have severely restricted their number and the scope of their activities.

Because of all these factors, the mix of American groups that have actually gone to China under the facilitated exchanges is quite different in important respects from what the principal exchange organizations and scholarly groups on the U.S. side originally hoped for. Apart from delegations from the three major American exchange organizations, the largest number of facilitated exchange groups going to China has consisted of persons specializing in scientific fields, such as medicine (including groups interested in acupuncture anesthesia, herbal pharmacology, and schistosomiasis), physics (including experts in solid-state physics), computer sciences, seismology, plant studies, and insect control. The much less numerous delegations representing the social sciences and humanities have included groups interested in art and archeology, early childhood development, linguistics, paleoanthropology, and rural small-scale industries. One U.S. performing arts group, the Philadelphia orchestra, and several sports teams, in swimming and diving, basketball, and track and field, have gone. In the broad field of education and public affairs, only three American groups have gone under the facilitated exchanges: a university presidents' delegation, a group of teachers, and a delegation representing American world affairs organizations. The number of people involved in these exchanges is infinitesimal compared to the number of Americans going to Japan or to European countries. The process of developing significant contacts, in short, has only just begun.

In negotiating the facilitated exchanges, although in the majority of cases both sides have avoided raising overt political issues, the Chinese in a few instances have deliberately chosen to do so. In 1974, for example, they vetoed an American scholar accompanying a linguistics delegation scheduled to go to China, charging (wrongly) that he had been a spy in China prior to the Communist takeover; they only backed down when it became clear that the delegation's visit would be canceled if they did not accept him. In 1975 they insisted that a Chinese performing arts group scheduled to visit the United States be permitted to sing a highly political song about "liberating Taiwan." Later in the year they vetoed on political grounds one member of a group of American mayors planning to go to China; he was the conservative mayor of San Juan, and the Chinese made no secret of the fact that this action reflected their sympathy for the Puerto Rican independence movement. In both of these cases the visits were ultimately canceled by the Americans because the Chinese were not willing to modify their politicized positions. From 1974 on, also, Chinese groups visiting the United States repeatedly protested any symbols of, or references to, the Nationalist regime that they encountered—inadvertently, as far as their American host organizations were concerned. The instances in which politics have intruded blatantly into the exchange process have not been extensive enough to undermine the existing facilitated exchange relationships, but they clearly have strained them on occasion, and in the eyes of American sponsors of exchanges they have raised troublesome questions about the future.

The overwhelming majority of Americans who have visited China have, in any case, gone outside the framework of the negotiated exchanges, on the direct invitation of the Chinese. The Chinese, with complete freedom to pick and choose, have focused special attention on the Overseas Chinese. Among these Americans of Chinese origin, Peking has tried to build a constituency favorably disposed to the People's Republic, partly for political reasons and partly to obtain their cooperation in various scientific, technical, and business fields. The Chinese have also worked hard to encourage and attract support from various other American groups and individuals who are demonstrably inclined to be strongly pro-Peking. In doing so, they have publicly endorsed and given preferential treatment (for example, in the issuance of visas) to a network of U.S.-China People's Friendship Associations. These have sprung up in recent years in many different parts of the United States, and they now number several dozen. In 1974 they were merged into a national organization.

The Chinese have also invited a carefully selected list of American congressmen from both major parties and both branches of congress. By the fall of 1975 at least nine congressional missions, including thirty-five congressmen had gone,[9] and more have gone since then. They have given visas to a sizable number of American news correspondents; however, the overwhelming majority of them have gone on very short trips, often in conjunction with visits by the secretary of state or the President. The Chinese have also granted visas to a growing number of U.S. businessmen, the majority of whom have been invited to attend the twice-yearly Canton trade fairs.

Clearly the exchanges developed so far have played a useful role in U.S.-China relations, both as a symbol of improving political relations and as a mechanism for initiating contacts between the two societies. Few Americans would question the value of continuing them, and there are

9. Frank Valeo, "Statement of the Secretary of the Senate," presented at the 1975 members' meeting of the National Committee on United States-China Relations (Oct. 29, 1975; processed), pp. 4–5.

good arguments for gradually expanding them, *if* this can be done on a mutually beneficial basis. But the *if* is important. It is essential from the U.S. perspective to remedy some of the asymmetries and shortcomings in existing arrangements and to move toward a pattern that serves both nations' interests in a balanced and effective way. Otherwise, it may be difficult to sustain the exchange relationships, even at their present level. However, if they can be improved, exchanges could make an increasingly important contribution to the strengthening of Sino-American relations.

The greatest need, aside from correcting obvious imbalances, is to make the contacts less superficial. While the Chinese have enjoyed considerable freedom, in dealing with the open and pluralistic society in the United States, to acquire new scientific and technical knowledge and attempt to influence U.S. public opinion (and, through it, U.S. policy), the Americans, in dealing with China's state-directed, disciplined, and relatively closed society, have had very limited opportunities to pursue objectives they consider important. Almost all Americans going to China have been restricted to what might be called brief familiarization visits— or, less charitably, "guided tours." Few Americans have been able to conduct genuine research. Moreover, the social scientists and humanists, who have the strongest desire for contacts, have clearly been discriminated against.[10] With minor exceptions, no American scholars have been able to spend extended periods at Chinese educational or research institutions. Nor have American students—again with minor exceptions—been permitted to attend Chinese educational institutions, even for language study. Contacts between American and Chinese, either in China or in the United States, have generally not led to lasting relationships of significance. American public affairs groups have rarely been able to engage the Chinese in serious discussions of controversial issues. And no American journalists have been granted permission to set up offices, or even make long visits, in China; Peking has stated explicitly, in fact, that it does not intend to allow them to do so until formal diplomatic relations are established.

Clearly, U.S. visitors to China cannot expect to have the kind of access to Chinese society that the United States allows Chinese visitors. Yet,

10. The Committee on Scholarly Communication has had little success in its persistent efforts to expand the number of delegations of American social scientists and humanists sent to China under facilitated exchanges. However, as of early 1976, Alex De Angelis of the committee staff had recorded a total of 661 known "scholarly travelers" of all sorts from the United States to China—231 of them social scientists, just over 300 of them social scientists plus humanists, and 125 of them specialists on Chinese affairs.

scientific, technical, educational, and cultural exchanges are the principal means whereby, gradually, mutually beneficial links can be created, increased mutual tolerance encouraged, and greater reciprocal knowledge and understanding achieved between important groups in the two societies. The aim of U.S. policy, therefore, should be to develop nonofficial contacts further, with the immediate emphasis on qualitative improvement. The United States should push for longer visits, both ways, by scientists and other scholars, permitting serious research and leading to follow-up contacts of lasting significance. It should propose Sino-American meetings and conferences in which a genuine interchange of ideas can occur, and joint research projects or parallel studies on problems of common interest. It should press for more visits to China both by social scientists and humanists and by public affairs groups composed of non-scholars. It should insist that both sides avoid trying to manipulate exchanges for short-term political advantages. It should propose a two-way exchange of students between U.S. and Chinese educational institutions, starting perhaps with students desiring to engage in language study. And it should urge the Chinese to permit some major U.S. press organizations to station regular correspondents in Peking for extended stays.

The Chinese cannot be expected suddenly to agree to do all of these things. They may insist that the establishment of normal diplomatic relations is a prerequisite to any expansion or improvement of exchanges. Even thereafter, changes are likely to be slow, at best. Those in China who most fear contamination and subversion from contacts with the outside world will doubtless continue to oppose such moves on political grounds. As long as China's "revolution in education" continues, moreover, universities and research institutions as well as individual scholars will be politically inhibited from establishing more meaningful relationships with foreign institutions and scholars, and in many instances they will be ill-equipped to do so even if they so desire. If recent political changes in China result in more pragmatic policies, which is possible, the outlook may improve, but one should not expect dramatic sudden changes.

Bridging the enormous intellectual, as well as ideological and political, barriers between the two societies will be an extremely difficult and long-term process, under even the best of circumstances. Nevertheless, the United States should persistently work to develop strong exchange relationships and try to persuade Peking that this would serve Chinese as well as American interests. Both the U.S. government and the private American institutions involved in exchanges can legitimately insist, also, that increased opportunities for Chinese to pursue their particular objectives through exchanges must be balanced by increased opportunities for Americans to pursue goals they believe are important. If such a balance can be achieved—but only if it can be achieved—exchanges should contribute significantly to a gradual deepening of relations between the two countries.

Military-Security Relations

Trade and exchanges have been the most visible aspects of the developing U.S.-China relationship (apart from presidential visits and Secretary of State Kissinger's periodic trips), and could in the long run be of substantial significance. However, many crucial questions concerning relations between the two countries have received less public attention; they concern military-security and arms control issues, which involve fundamental questions of war or peace.

Today the United States and China have no formal relationships in these fields. There are no explicit links, or negotiations, between Washington and Peking on bilateral military problems or arms control. Nevertheless a security relationship does exist, implicitly, as it must between any two great powers whose interests and policies intersect. Moreover, in the future, issues involving military security and arms control will have to be dealt with more explicitly and directly.

The most fundamental change in relations between the United States and China in recent years has been the transformation from a pattern of hostile military confrontation to one of military restraint and cautious accommodation. But the character of the present military-security relationship is difficult to define, and determining future U.S. policy requires analysis of some extremely delicate and sensitive issues.

Even though both the United States and China have taken steps to minimize the dangers of military conflict, the two countries are obviously not allies, and neither is likely to view the relationship in traditional alliance terms in the foreseeable future. In fact, neither can ignore the possibilities for future Sino-American conflict.

Nevertheless, in regard to security issues their policies today involve certain elements of parallelism and even of tacit cooperation. One key question for the United States is whether it should push that parallelism further. Another is whether it should try to develop direct military links and cooperate overtly with the Chinese on matters involving military security.[11] In attempting to deal with such questions, it is important to define the basic assumptions and objectives that should underlie U.S. policy. This requires an appraisal of what American military analysts refer to as the "China threat" as well as the arguments for and against future parallelism or cooperation with the Chinese in military matters.

To date, China has never had, and it still lacks, any capability to pose a direct military threat—nuclear or conventional, air or naval—to the United States itself.[12] If it develops an operational force of intercontinental ballistic missiles (ICBMs), it may be capable of inflicting nuclear damage on the United States; but China's vulnerability to massive retaliation should prevent rational Chinese leaders, with adequate control over their missile forces, from posing threats against the United States itself, although China could threaten a small retaliatory strike in the event of an American attack.

China does have a theoretical capability to pose a nuclear threat, but not at present a significant conventional threat, against Japan, the United States' major ally in Asia. But unless there are far-reaching changes in the entire East Asian situation as well as in Peking's basic policies, it is implausible that Chinese leaders would consider posing such a threat; even if they were to consider doing so, they should be effectively deterred from actually using nuclear weapons, so long as the U.S.-Japan security treaty provides Tokyo with a dependable "nuclear umbrella."

China obviously can pose a substantial threat with its conventional military forces to the smaller nations on its periphery, including some that have close relationships with the United States. There is no evidence, however, that it now plans such actions. In the context of its current overall foreign policy and the present general situation in East Asia it seems unlikely to do so. Peking's past intervention in Korea and involvement in Vietnam were in response to U.S. actions that it saw as threatening to China. In the period ahead, even if China's new leaders are tempted to use force against small neighbors, they will be strongly inhibited from doing so by the potential dangers from retaliatory responses from either the Soviet Union or the United States, and the political and economic

11. Among the few scholarly analyses of this question is Michael Pillsbury, "U.S.-Chinese Military Ties?" *Foreign Policy*, no. 20 (Fall 1975), pp. 50–64.

12. For background on China's military capabilities, see Angus M. Fraser, *The People's Liberation Army, Communist China's Armed Forces* (New York: Crane Russak, 1973); and International Institute for Strategic Studies, *The Military Balance, 1974–75* (London: IISS, 1974).

costs that military adventurism could incur. It is reasonable to assume, therefore, that despite China's capabilities, there is a low probability at present of China initiating major military actions even against vulnerable nations on its periphery.

One of the principal dangers the United States must consider in assessing a China threat, however, is the possible initiation of military action by North Korea or North Vietnam. China maintains important military relations with, and provides significant military support to, these two Communist "middle powers." If either of them precipitated a local conflict, China might provide them with support, and an enlarged conflict could draw in other major powers, including the United States.

China also is capable of providing military support to insurrectionary movements in nearby countries. It seems unlikely, however, that Peking will consider direct Chinese military intervention to aid such movements. In fact, Peking will probably limit even its covert support in the period immediately ahead, unless either the general regional situation or basic Chinese policies change.

At present, therefore, American leaders can and should take a relatively relaxed view of any potential "China threat." On its part, the United States should avoid military deployments and policies that might again heighten Chinese fears of a U.S. threat. Nevertheless, for political as well as military reasons, it should continue to maintain a military presence in East Asia. At present the necessity for this derives less from any imminent danger of major Chinese military action directed either against American forces or against allies of the United States, than from the need to deter Moscow from increasing its military activity in the area, to psychologically reassure U.S. allies and other small nations in the region and help bolster their capacity to deal with internal insurrections or local conflicts, to help deter the medium-sized Communist powers from considering reckless military actions, and to create a more stable equilibrium among the major powers in the region. In addition, a continuing U.S. military presence should reinforce Chinese prudence and restraint and insure against the possibility of a future change in Chinese policies.

The existing strategic capabilities of U.S. naval, air, and missile forces assigned to the region will be sufficient to deter any nuclear threat even after China acquires ICBMs. And although the strength of U.S. conventional units in the area has been substantially reduced recently, they are also probably sufficient to meet U.S. obligations (and will continue to be so even with some further adjustments downward). In Korea U.S. forces help both to deter North Korea and counterbalance its air superiority and to prevent provocative action on the part of the South. In Japan and the Philippines, U.S. bases provide a symbol of U.S. defense commitments and support for U.S. naval and air forces, which have an important stabilizing role throughout East Asia. Even though it is highly unlikely— and generally so recognized—that the United States will intervene with its own military forces in Southeast Asia in the years immediately ahead, U.S. military support of noncommunist nations, along with political and economic aid, continues to be a significant factor in the region and contributes to the strategic balance in important ways.

Since the start of the 1970s, the context in which security issues in East Asia must be viewed has broadened. Problems now cannot be approached simply in terms of combating, deterring, or containing any one threatening power, whether it be China or the Soviet Union. The maintenance and stabilization of the general equilibrium in the region have become the prime task. Policies designed to achieve broad political and economic deterrence—policies aimed at making major aggressive action excessively costly in political and economic as well as military terms— are likely to be at least as important as those aimed at military deterrence per se.

Even though neither the United States nor China can exclude the possibility of future military conflict between themselves, and must therefore be prepared to cope with that contingency, this is not a preoccupation today in either capital. In fact, there is an increasing tendency on both sides to focus attention on elements of possible parallelism or convergence in their military-security concerns and interests.

Though the parallelism that has developed is largely tacit, and clearly limited, it is important because it concerns U.S. and Chinese relations with the other major powers in East Asia. Both Washington and Peking oppose increases in the Soviet military presence and power position in East Asia, as well as in South Asia or other adjacent regions such as the Middle East. China's fear of Russia's actions, especially in East Asia, may be more acute than that of the United States, but the two have common interests in regard to the problem.

Both Washington and Peking also oppose major remilitarization by Japan—especially Japan's development of a nuclear capability. Here again, however, the motives and concerns of the two differ despite the elements of convergence. Washington believes that a nonmilitarized Japan, without nuclear arms, can in cooperation with the United States play a major constructive role in Asia and globally and that the remilitarization of Japan would have unfortunate political effects within Japan and could tend to destabilize the regional equilibrium, creating alarm throughout East Asia and perhaps weakening, or even undermining, the U.S.-Japan relationship. China's major concern is that a Japan without any security link to the United States might tilt toward the Soviet Union. Peking's latent long-range concern is that a rearmed Japan could become aggressive and pose a direct threat to China once again.

Despite the differences in their motivations, both countries are now inclined to use their influence, in parallel at least, to discourage any moves by the Soviet Union aimed at increasing its military role in the region—for example, efforts to expand its naval activities in Southeast Asia or to acquire base rights in the region. And in striking contrast to the recent past, China now approves the maintenance of the U.S. military alliance with Japan and favors a significant U.S. military presence in other areas of potential conflict in East Asia where a U.S. withdrawal could create a military vacuum into which the Soviet Union might move. The Chinese doubtless still believe that eventually all non-Asian powers should get entirely out of the region, militarily, but not under existing circumstances. Today, instead of being primarily concerned that the United States will continue a military presence in East Asia, they appear more concerned that it may not be willing or able to play a strong enough role to check the rise of Soviet influence. Their position obviously could change if their fears of Moscow's intentions abated. But, for the present, the Chinese are deliberately forgoing opportunities to use their influence to weaken the American military position in East Asia and exert pressure for rapid U.S. withdrawals—for example, in their dealings with the Thais and Filipinos—and are communicating to the United States, often indirectly and elliptically, their desire that Washington not weaken its military position. The main Chinese fear at present focuses on the possible political consequences of apparent shifts in the military balance. Thus the political effects of the U.S. military presence are especially important.

Peking's interest in a continuing military role for the United States in East Asia may be ironical, but it is an important fact that alters the basic situation, for continuation of a significant and credible U.S. military role has become a positive force in the development of U.S.-China relations. If the United States were to withdraw militarily, or the credibility of its military role in the region were undermined, China's view of its stake in the Sino-American relationship might significantly diminish.

The kind of parallelism that exists today in the U.S.-China security relationship does not yet involve, and does not require, overt military cooperation. It is very possible, however, that in the period immediately ahead either Washington or Peking could seriously consider whether, and if so how and to what extent, the two countries should establish direct military contacts.

There were hints from the Chinese side, in conversations with non-official Americans during 1974–75, of possible interest in purchases of U.S. military technology. There were also articles in the Chinese press indicating that at least some leaders in Peking argued for obtaining advanced military technology from abroad,[13] and China began to purchase important military items from other Western countries.[14] However, when a congressional delegation consisting mainly of House Armed Services Committee members visited China in April 1976, the Chinese did not express any interest in obtaining U.S. arms.[15]

In the United States, public discussion of the issue, which began in late 1975,[16] increased in early 1976. Statements by former Defense Secretary James Schlesinger that there had been discussion in the U.S. government of whether to consider arms sales to China evoked statements by State Department officials that the issue had not been discussed "specifically."[17] A short time later, Commerce Department Secretary Elliot L. Richardson was reported to have said publicly that the United States would be willing to discuss arms sales to China if Peking raised the subject.[18]

Though such mixed signals give no indication of how seriously the issues are being considered by the two governments, they do argue for public consideration of the policy questions involved. The issues, clearly, are of extraordinary sensitivity. Any moves toward an explicit military

13. See "Wei Yuan's Thought Against Aggression," in *Selections*, pp. 1–14. The article, discussing a historical case, obviously favors "studying the strong points of foreign countries," "mastering the strong points of the barbarians in order to overpower them," specifically applying this to arms and military technology as well as to science and economic technology.

14. *New York Times*, Nov. 10 and Dec. 18, 1975.

15. Ibid., April 26, 1976.

16. Pillsbury, "U.S.-Chinese Military Ties?" stimulated a flurry of interest; see *Newsweek*, Sept. 8, 1975, p. 15, and Dec. 8, 1975, p. 38; *Washington Post*, Oct. 9, 1975; *New York Times*, Oct. 15, 1975; *Time*, Oct. 20, 1975, p. 33; and *Economist*, Oct. 18, 1975, p. 15. For Russian reactions, see *Foreign Broadcast Information Service Daily Report—USSR*, Oct. 28, 1975, p. C-2, and Oct. 31, 1975, p. C-2.

17. *Washington Post*, April 12, 1976.

18. Ibid., May 29, 1976.

relationship could have far-reaching consequences for U.S. relations with the Soviet Union and Japan as well as China; they will obviously have to be dealt with by the United States with the utmost of caution and prudence.

If at some point the Chinese decide to explore the possibilities, they probably will focus attention first on access to information about U.S. military technology, then later on the possibility of purchasing military equipment. Whether China should move toward military contacts with the United States will almost certainly be a highly controversial issue in China. Some Chinese leaders can be expected to oppose the idea strongly, on ideological and political grounds. Others, however, may favor it, for strictly pragmatic reasons.

The most obvious Chinese motive for deciding to extend serious feelers for contacts in this field would be the actual desire to obtain much-needed information on advanced weapons technology, or prototypes, or limited supplies of certain military equipment that would enable them to close some of the great gaps between Chinese and Soviet military capabilities. But some Chinese leaders might hope also to lay the groundwork for a much more extensive cooperation that could directly involve the United States in the event of a Soviet attack on China. And it is possible that the primary objectives behind Chinese feelers could be psychological and political—a desire deliberately to arouse Russian fears of Sino-American collusion, to create new sources of U.S.-Soviet frictions, possibly to complicate U.S. relations with other nations. The United States will have to make some very difficult judgments about Chinese motives in considering its own policy. It will also have to weigh the possible consequences, direct and indirect, of whatever it decides to do.

It is possible to argue on strictly military grounds that it is desirable for China not only to be able to defend itself against possible Soviet threats but also to tie down Soviet forces in the East, and that because China is now so vulnerable, U.S. interests would be well-served by actively helping Peking to strengthen its defensive capabilities. Even though Moscow would doubtless object, it would have few legitimate reasons for doing so because it now enjoys such overwhelming military superiority over Peking. Conceivably, a less unequal balance in the military strength of the two Communist powers might increase the stability of their relationship and therefore reduce the dangers of conflict in East Asia. Moreover, Moscow's uncertainty about the possibility of U.S. military support of China in the event of conflict might increase its inhibitions against considering military action against China. In terms of U.S.

military strategy globally, any policies that compelled Moscow to station large military forces in East Asia could be advantageous. And even very limited military cooperation with the United States might encourage China to forgo, or at least postpone, development of intercontinental and submarine-launched ballistic missiles designed to reach U.S. targets.

Some sort of military cooperation could also be viewed as a means of increasing Peking's stake in the overall U.S.-China relationship and reducing the possibility that it will consider other policy options, including the reestablishment of military relations with Moscow. As a quid pro quo for military cooperation, perhaps Peking might make significant political concessions and show increased political restraint in dealings with the United States. Some who consider a far-reaching Sino-Soviet reapprochement as a real danger feel the risks of that occurring could be significantly reduced if the United States established some sort of military link with China.

Despite all such arguments, however, there will also be many arguments against developing overt Sino-American cooperation in the military field; it might have varied undesirable, unwanted, and potentially dangerous consequences and conceivably could involve serious risks. Any U.S.-China military link might be the first step down a "slippery slope" of U.S. involvement in problems and conflicts it should stay out of. China's internal politics and its leadership are still so unpredictable that the possibility of a reversion by the Chinese to hostile policies cannot be ruled out. Therefore, any improvement of China's military capabilities might simply increase Peking's ability to threaten U.S. allies and other noncommunist countries in Asia.

The strongest argument against steps toward a direct U.S.-China military relationship is the possibility that it would have seriously adverse effects on the pattern of relationships among the major powers in East Asia, especially those of the Soviet Union with the United States and China. If it confirmed Moscow's fears about anti-Soviet collusion by Washington and Peking, Soviet paranoia could heighten, Sino-Soviet tensions increase, and conceivably Soviet pressures on China become more severe. Chinese leaders, rather than becoming more reasonable, might adopt a more intransigent, or provocative, stance. The adverse effects on U.S.-Soviet relations could be destabilizing. And the U.S. alliance with Japan could be weakened if many Japanese came to question the basic priorities of U.S. policy in East Asia. If Tokyo's apprehensions about China's military capabilities should increase, the influence of those in

Japan who favor Japanese remilitarization might also grow. Any evidence of U.S.-China military cooperation is likely also to stir latent fears of China in the smaller Asian nations.

The United States cannot ignore the risk of destabilizing the overall big-power equilibrium in East Asia by establishing military links with China. Those who minimize this risk can, it is true, cite a variety of past instances in which complex but limited military relationships were established without producing any of the theoretically possible disastrous results—for example, U.S. military aid to Yugoslavia after 1948 to bolster its defenses against possible Soviet threats despite Moscow's displeasure; Soviet military aid to Cuba after 1962 (other than nuclear missiles) despite continuing U.S. disapproval; Washington's arms sales to various Arab countries despite the possibility that those arms could be used against the U.S.-supported regime in Israel; and the symbolically important exchange visits of Rumanian and Chinese military delegations, despite Moscow's obvious disapproval. Yet none of these is really analogous, for the U.S.-Chinese-Soviet triangle is unique in many respects, and the dangers of destabilizing the existing relationships in East Asia are much greater.

If the question of establishing U.S.-China military cooperation were to arise in black and white, either/or terms, all the pertinent factors could be weighed simultaneously in deciding what U.S. policy should be. The problem is more likely, however, to arise in many different guises, starting with proposals for relatively small moves, often involving subtle and ambiguous issues. The larger issue could be obscured. Calculating the potential gains and risks of small moves may be extremely difficult; and it would be a mistake to judge them on their own merits alone, without considering whether they might be the first steps leading to an escalating U.S. involvement.

If the United States is to engage in a process of direct interaction of any sort with the Chinese in the military field, it must have a fairly clear idea of where it will draw the line and stop. Before making any specific moves, therefore, it would be wise to determine not only what steps might be worth considering under existing circumstances, but also those that Washington should clearly refuse to consider, and some of the possibilities that fall between the two extremes.

Some of the initial questions will focus on whether there should be military contact of any sort. For example, should there be conversations between American and Chinese officers or military leaders? If so, in

China or the United States? Or in third countries? Should military delegations be exchanged? Should the two countries accept military attachés from each other after formal diplomatic relations have been established?

Another set of questions will concern the possibilities of the United States sharing information or selling equipment to China that could be militarily useful. Should the United States sell to China, for civilian purposes, technology and equipment that could easily have military uses—for example, computers, jet transports, or helicopters? Should Washington make available intelligence information that it knows China would find useful in planning its defenses—for example, information on general Soviet military capabilities and deployments, and possibly on Soviet missile firings? Should it go further and develop channels for sharing certain types of intelligence data exclusively with China?

Other questions will concern more explicit, though still limited, forms of military cooperation. Should the United States sell to China technological information that is clearly military in its utility but relatively unsophisticated? Should it also make available prototypes of military equipment, or sell limited quantities of equipment? If sales are considered, should they be restricted to items principally useful for passive defense, such as data or equipment useful in communications, satellite reconnaissance, antisubmarine sonar, and early warning radar?

Eventually, questions might be raised about whether the United States should be prepared to sell information or military items that could clearly be used to improve Chinese offensive capabilities, such as technology useful for the development of offensive long-range aircraft or missiles, even though the Russians would obviously view this as extremely dangerous. Finally, if a military relationship develops, questions would probably be eventually raised about whether the United States should be prepared to sell large quantities of equipment of any of the types mentioned to China.

These questions are worth raising if for no other reason than to highlight the fact that once any direct military links are established between the United States and China, the door may be open to a much more far-reaching military relationship. This obviously argues for caution on the U.S. part about starting down this road. I believe that a prudent and sensible position for the United States to adopt at present regarding U.S.-China military contacts and cooperation would be to firmly close the door to certain possibilities, study certain others without making any moves now to implement them, and indicate that Washington is prepared now to consider, cautiously, only certain very limited steps. At present, the United States should show its willingness to establish contacts to discuss military as well as political and economic problems, if China is seriously interested. It should also, however, make clear to Peking that a primary U.S. consideration in whatever it does is its desire to avoid actions that might significantly increase tensions or destabilize big-power relations in East Asia.

Under present circumstances, the United States should firmly close the door to sales to China of any equipment or technology that is useful above all for advanced offensive weapons systems, and also to large-scale sales of military equipment of any sort. The repercussions of making such sales—in the Soviet Union, Japan, and elsewhere—would be such as to make them unwise, even though they might do no more than reduce China's military inferiority. Moreover, the present state of U.S.-China relations, and uncertainties about the future of the relationship, are such that sales of this sort are simply not justifiable.

The United States can leave open, however, and study, further, the possibility of exchanging intelligence information bilaterally; if such exchanges are considered, however, they should be restricted to information useful primarily for defensive and not offensive purposes (a difficult line to determine). Another possibility that need not be totally excluded at this point, although it would have more far-reaching consequences and risks and obviously could not be undertaken lightly, would be providing data, and possibly prototypes, for military items useful for improving China's passive defense systems. One can also imagine circumstances in which the United States might also wish to consider selling to China limited quantities of relatively unsophisticated conventional military hardware, which could enhance its defensive capabilities without significantly increasing its anti-Soviet or anti-U.S. offensive potential (another difficult-to-draw line). Today a careful balancing of the pros and cons of taking such steps argues against them, in my view, but the calculus of benefits and costs could change, and the United States need not foreclose the option of considering such steps at some point in the future. They would be aimed at helping China improve its passive defense capabilities, without unduly enhancing its offensive military capabilities. They should only be seriously considered, however, if the United States were satisfied that the trend in its relations with China was toward continued improvement, thereby minimizing the risk of future U.S.-China conflict; that Peking was prepared to be less provocative in its dealings with Moscow, thereby reducing the risk of Sino-Soviet conflict; and that Washington could convince the Russians that China's strengthened defense would not create a serious military threat to the Soviet Union.

The caution that should govern American sales of military hardware to China need not apply to the same extent to U.S. allies in Europe. Britain, Germany, France, and conceivably even Japan may make sales of items such as defensive fighter aircraft, which the United States should not oppose even though it restricts U.S. sales of similar items. European sales would involve fewer risks of destabilizing relations with Moscow (although neither the United States nor the other members of the North Atlantic Treaty Organization should assume that there would be no risks at all involved). During the past two years China has purchased some military items from Europe, and the U.S. government has, in effect, given tacit approval to such sales.[19] This is a sensible policy under the circumstances of today.

The principal step that the United States itself should consider in the near future is a very limited one: namely, the establishment of direct contacts between American and Chinese military personnel. There clearly would be value in initiating discussions between military officers, and after the establishment of diplomatic relations in exchanging military attachés. (The United States, China, and the Soviet Union all routinely develop contacts of this kind with adversaries as well as friends.)

19. In December 1975 after long negotiations with British Rolls-Royce representatives the Chinese received a license to manufacture the Spey engine (*Washington Post* and *New York Times*, Dec. 15, 1975). The engines can clearly be used for defensive military aircraft; yet Britain gave no indication that it intended to ask COCOM (the intergovernmental coordinating committee through which the major noncommunist nations have coordinated trade policies affecting strategic items) for permission to make an agreement, nor did the United States appear to try to block its implementation.

Shortly thereafter, West Germany's Messerschmitt-Bolkow-Blohn group was reported to be negotiating a licensing agreement for the manufacture in China of its B-105 helicopter (*U.S.-China Business Review*, January–February 1976, p. 52).

On December 28, 1975, *Sankei*, a leading Japanese newspaper, reported that the Chinese were showing a strong interest in purchasing Japanese-manufactured US-1 amphibious patrol and sea rescue planes (*Daily Summary of Japanese Press*, Jan. 8, 1976, p. 32). The paper commented that such a sale would be "a breakthrough for our country's export of weapons"; no agreement had been reached, however, and strong opposition was expected both in and out of the government.

The Chinese have purchased some French helicopters. There have been reports of their interest in purchasing (and possibly licensing for manufacture) the French Mirage fighter; in January 1976, however, in conversations with French officials at the Foreign Ministry in Paris, I was unable to obtain official confirmation of this.

In addition, Washington should seriously consider the possibility of publicly releasing intelligence data—for example data that it obtains from satellites—that are already available to Moscow but not to Peking and that would be useful to China in a defensive sense. And the United States should follow a policy that minimizes security restrictions on technology and equipment that are on the borderline between civilian and military use and that would therefore permit the sale of certain types of computers, transport jets, helicopters, and the like. (Even the Soviet Union has continued to sell transport jets and helicopters to China, despite the intensity of the Sino-Soviet dispute.)

To sum up, the keynote of any U.S. approach to the establishment of direct military relations with China at present should be caution. Washington should view sympathetically China's problem of improving its defense capabilities in the face of the Soviet Union's vastly superior military power, and it should actively throw its political weight into the balance to help deter any Sino-Soviet military conflict provoked by either side. But the United States cannot ignore the extreme sensitivity of the U.S.-China-Soviet military triangle and should avoid actions that might have destabilizing effects on existing relationships. It must not ignore possible repercussions elsewhere in Asia, especially in Japan, and it should consult closely with Tokyo on these as on other major policy issues. Even though the United States can now, without undue risks or costs, consider establishing military contacts with China, pursuing a liberal policy on technology transfers, and maintaining a tolerant position on European military sales to China, it should not itself engage in direct sales of purely military technology or hardware to Peking. While pursuing a policy of prudence in this respect, however, it need not completely close the door to sales in the future of technology and hardware useful primarily for passive defense systems.

All in all, the issues in this field are so complex and sensitive that they demand continuing study. All the potential ramifications, both political and military, of any moves the United States might make must be carefully considered, and in the meantime precipitous steps should be avoided.

Arms Control

Another critically important set of issues that the United States must confront in its dealings with China in the years immediately ahead relates to arms control.[20] Over the long run, the success or failure in promoting arms control measures affecting East Asia, and in engaging China as well as other major nations in the process, will be a basic determinant of the prospects for peace and stability in the region.

It will be extremely difficult to find a basis for discourse and agreement in this field, however. Today, the prospects are not favorable for serious discussions between Washington and Peking on arms control; on many of the key issues the basic attitudes of the two countries are vastly different. The United States will doubtless have to take the initiative in raising arms control issues with the Chinese. Peking's long-standing opposition to the dominance of the two superpowers in arms control and its reluctance to associate itself in any way with measures that it has consistently attacked in the past may well lead it to resist even the opening of a dialogue.

It is possible to argue that because of the immense gap between the two nations' positions and interests relating to arms control, it is unrealistic and perhaps even undesirable at present to try to open a serious dialogue. Chinese participation is not now essential for the immediate success of the most important U.S.-Soviet efforts to reach agreements in the Strategic Arms Limitation Talks, and in view of China's opposition to these and many other international arms control efforts, involvement of China now might simply complicate existing problems. But to argue that it would be desirable to count China out until Peking adopts a more cooperative and constructive approach is simplistic and short-sighted.

Clearly, China's participation will be essential in the future, and perhaps in the not distant future, when China's nuclear arsenal is larger. Already, China's noncooperation raises serious problems in connection with certain existing arms control efforts, and China's cooperation on other questions would be extremely helpful. It should not be assumed, moreover, that China will refuse indefinitely to become involved in all significant international arms control efforts. Even today, while denouncing virtually every U.S.-Soviet agreement, China is, in fact, in-

20. For a more detailed discussion, see Ralph N. Clough, A. Doak Barnett, Morton H. Halperin, and Jerome H. Kahan, *The United States, China, and Arms Control* (Brookings Institution, 1975). Other recent analyses include Harry Gelber, *Nuclear Weapons and Chinese Policy*, Adelphi Papers, no. 99 (London: International Institute for Strategic Studies, 1973); and Jonathan D. Pollack, "China and the Politics of Arms Control" (paper prepared for the annual meeting of the International Studies Association, February 1976; processed).

volved in a variety of ways, both explicitly and tacitly, in the field of arms control. It has, itself, for example, unilaterally put forward a variety of proposals; although many are primarily propagandistic, they should not be ignored. More important, to a limited extent China has begun to play a role in certain international arms control discussions and even to endorse some kinds of international agreements.

Despite the obvious problems of trying to persuade the Chinese that it is genuinely in their interest to become much more broadly and constructively involved in international arms control efforts, this should be an important goal of U.S. policy during the next few years. Engaging the Chinese in this field must be viewed as a long-term process, but the United States and others should begin to work patiently and persistently toward this goal.

In order to define reasonable and realistic U.S. goals, it is necessary to try to understand Chinese motives, attitudes, and policies. The current official Chinese stand on arms control is summarized in recent speeches by Chinese leaders. In one of the most succinct, given to the United Nations on October 2, 1974, Vice Foreign Minister Ch'iao Kuan-hua (who later served as foreign minister, until December 1976) declared:

Disarmament is an old issue. And China's views on it are well known. We are in favor of disarmament. But we favor genuine and not sham disarmament, still less empty talk about disarmament coupled with actual arms expansion year after year . . . the convening of a nominal disarmament conference or its preparatory meeting will only produce the objective effect of lulling the people of the world. The Chinese government is in favor of holding a genuine world disarmament conference. But the conference must have a clear aim and the necessary preconditions. The clear aim is the complete prohibition and thorough destruction of nuclear weapons, and absolutely not the so-called limitation of strategic arms. The necessary pre-conditions are: All nuclear countries and particularly the two nuclear superpowers, the Soviet Union and the United States, must first of all undertake the unequivocal obligation that at no time and in no circumstances will they be the first to use nuclear weapons, particularly against non-nuclear countries and nuclear-free zones . . . and they must withdraw from abroad all their armed forces, including nuclear missile forces, and dismantle all their military bases, including nuclear bases, on the territories of other countries. Only thus will it be possible for all countries big and small, on an equal footing, to discuss with equanimity and resolve the question of the complete prohibition and thorough destruction of nuclear weapons and other questions free from any threat of force.[21]

21. *Peking Review*, Oct. 11, 1974, p. 14.

Elsewhere in his speech Ch'iao reiterated the Chinese unilateral no-first-use pledge, made initially in 1964 when China exploded its first nuclear device:

The Chinese Government has solemnly declared on many occasions that at no time and under no circumstances will China be the first to use nuclear weapons. It consistently holds that the nuclear countries should undertake not to use or threaten to use nuclear weapons against non-nuclear countries or nuclear-free zones.[22]

China places considerable importance on the desirability of establishing nuclear-free zones. It has formally signed a commitment to honor the Latin American nuclear-free zone; it currently supports proposals for such zones in South Asia, the Middle East, and Africa; and in the past it has proposed an Asian and Pacific nuclear-free zone.

As Ch'iao's speech indicates, however, the Chinese officially oppose, in very broad terms, one of the fundamental concepts underlying arms control, that is, the proposition that there is value in partial measures designed to stabilize existing military situations and balances and that they are probably a prerequisite for efforts to reduce armaments. Ch'iao dismissed arms control as "so-called limitations of strategic arms." Peking endorses, instead, total disarmament in the strategic weapons field and insists that the aim must be "the complete prohibition and thorough destruction of nuclear weapons," an aim that most Western leaders and specialists consider to be utopian and unattainable. The Chinese also lay down some far-reaching preconditions for a world conference to discuss disarmament, including generalized no-first-use pledges by all the nuclear powers and the withdrawal of all foreign forces and closing of all foreign bases throughout the world.

In practice, however, China does not rigidly adhere to these positions, or reject all partial arms control measures. Even its official statements indicate this. For example, China's unilateral no-first-use pledge is an arms control measure of sorts. Of course, the primary motivation behind this pledge could be China's desire to deter the major nuclear powers from considering preemptive strikes while China is still relatively weak, and since the pledge is not reinforced or guaranteed by any international agreement, it could easily be unilaterally abandoned (once China's own nuclear strength is greater). Nevertheless, the significance of the pledge should not be dismissed out of hand. It is quite possible, also, that the measures China now lists as preconditions for a world disarmament con-

22. Ibid.

ference—for example, no-first-use pledges, and the withdrawal of foreign forces and bases—are not unchangeable but could be subject to
international negotiation; the list's main significance is that it indicates
the kinds of measures that are of particular interest to Peking at present.

Nevertheless, China's consistency in attacking the majority of past
international arms control agreements, and especially those based on
U.S. and Soviet initiatives, is discouraging, and obviously works against
U.S. interests and goals. The actual damage done by Peking's denunciations is not great, but Chinese opposition undeniably complicates the
search for progress in the arms control field.

China strongly opposes the Strategic Arms Limitation Talks (SALT)
which were begun in late 1969, and it has denounced all the agreements
resulting from them, including the 1972 agreement to restrict antiballistic
missiles (ABMs) and the 1974 agreement to negotiate ceilings on U.S.
and Soviet strategic missiles. The Chinese emphasize that these have not
yet produced any significant "disarmament." They also charge that the
agreements are designed simply to perpetuate the superpowers' "nuclear
monopoly." In other words, the Chinese say, existing U.S.-Soviet agreements merely codify the arms race and perpetuate the superpowers'
superiority.

To date, China has shown no serious interest in participating in the
Geneva Conference of the Committee on Disarmament (CCD), and it
opposes any general world disarmament conference unless far-reaching
preconditions are met. It has vehemently denounced the 1963 limited
test ban treaty, and it opposes proposals for a comprehensive test ban.
It argues that both of these, like other bilateral U.S.-Soviet agreements,
are simply devices to guarantee the superpowers' "nuclear hegemony"
and ensure the continued inferiority of all other nations, including China.
Chinese denunciations of the nonproliferation treaty are similar; the
treaty restricts others, Peking charges, without affecting the level of U.S.
and Soviet arms. China opposes the 1972 treaty banning biological warfare, asserting that since it did not ban chemical weapons too, it was
actually a step backward from the 1925 Geneva Protocol. (It remains,
however, to be seen what position China will finally adopt in regard to
the proposed convention banning chemical warfare.) China also opposes
the existing outer space and seabed treaties, which deal, in any case, with
problems fairly remote from China's most pressing concerns.

Despite its denunciation of the SALT talks, China has clearly benefited
from one result they produced. The U.S.-Soviet agreement not to build

large ABM systems forestalled programs in both countries that would have made it more difficult for China to acquire a credible nuclear deterrent. In effect, Washington and Moscow decided to rely on deterrence in dealing with China, as with each other, and this clearly made it easier for Peking to foresee the day when it could deal with them on similar terms. However, the Chinese are right in judging that the SALT agreements have not in any significant way reduced the vast nuclear superiority that both superpowers enjoy.

China's noninvolvement in SALT does not today pose any significant threat to the viability of the U.S.-Soviet agreements, but if Washington and Moscow attempt to agree on reductions of strategic arms, assuming Peking's nuclear arsenal continues to grow, the triangular nuclear relationship among these three nations will become more complex and delicate. At some point Chinese involvement, or at least tacit acquiesence or cooperation, will probably be essential.

The minimal accomplishments of the Geneva Conference of the Committee on Disarmament so far mean that neither China's interests nor the CCD's effectiveness have yet been greatly affected by China's nonmembership. This could change, however, if the CCD were to become more active. The CCD's members seem likely to conclude in time that to deal effectively with many arms control problems, it is necessary to involve China in their deliberations, even though this will unquestionably create some new complications. Probably, for example, the chairmanship of the committee would have to be made a rotating one involving China.

China's opposition to the limited test ban treaty (as well as the proposed comprehensive test ban) and in particular the nonproliferation treaty has unquestionably been harmful to the antiproliferation cause. Although it is difficult to judge its effects exactly, China's opposition has certainly had a generally negative effect on the attitudes of other nations; it has disturbed leaders in certain other nations, helped to reinforce attitudes in some places that discourage total renunciation of the nuclear option, and worked generally against the goal of universal acceptance of nonproliferation.

However, while China has refused openly to oppose proliferation, and at times has even endorsed the spread of nuclear weapons, it has nevertheless followed a tacit nonproliferation policy. There is no evidence that it has transferred any nuclear weapons data to any other nation, and it has reportedly turned down specific requests for nuclear weapons. Today, Chinese leaders state that they "don't practice it [pro-liferation] and don't encourage it" but are "not afraid of it."[23] This sug-gests that at least some of China's leaders recognize the dangers of pro-liferation, privately, if not publicly; and they doubtless do not wish to see countries such as Japan, to say nothing of regimes such as those in South Korea and Taiwan, acquire nuclear arms. India's explosion of a nuclear device may have highlighted the possibilities of further pro-liferation, in Chinese eyes, even though Peking deprecates the signifi-cance of the Indian explosion. In actuality, China has benefited from the nonproliferation treaty, despite the fact that it officially denounces it.

This is certainly not the case, however, with the limited test ban, or the proposed comprehensive test ban. Peking regarded the signing of the limited test ban treaty as a deliberate U.S.-Soviet attempt to prevent China from becoming a nuclear power, and it can be expected to continue opposing any measures that would restrict or constrain its own efforts to develop a significant nuclear arsenal. It is conceivable that Peking may eventually change its position; international disapproval, especially of atmospheric testing, could eventually have some effect on Chinese attitudes. But this will certainly not be for some time, until the Chinese are more confident about their own nuclear deterrent.

Although the Chinese have opposed the treaty banning biological warfare, they can probably be expected to adhere to its requirements. In fact in 1952 Peking ratified the 1925 Geneva Protocol, banning both bacteriological and chemical weapons, and this was its first formal en-dorsement of an international arms control agreement. (The Nationalist-ruled Republic of China had ratified the treaty in 1929.) It is conceiv-able that Peking would consider endorsing a new treaty banning chemi-cal warfare, if it were actively involved—as it should be—in negotiating it. Participation in such negotiations in the future could definitely affect Chinese attitudes; all of the treaties the Chinese have opposed were negotiated without their participation.

The reasons for, and motives underlying China's generally negative approach to arms control are complicated, yet in some respects they are understandable. The fact that China aspires to great-power status, yet continues in strategic terms to be weak and vulnerable, relative to the two superpowers, is one fundamental explanation. Chinese resent-

23. Report of an interview with Teng Hsiao-p'ing, in Phillips Talbot, "The Presi-dent's Letter, Views from Peking," in *Asia* (Asia Society newsletter), vol. 3, no. 1 (January–February 1976), p. 1.

ment of U.S. and Soviet leadership in the initiation of most major arms control proposals is another. In addition, there is considerable justification for the Chinese view that since none of the measures agreed upon reduces the gap in power between the two superpowers and weaker nations, their value to China is questionable. Peking is clearly still determined to improve China's defensive position, and it opposes—at this stage at least—anything that would restrict its ability to do so.

Chinese nonparticipation in the actual negotiation of past arms control agreements has also argued, in Chinese eyes, against adherence. In addition, China has regarded many arms control issues as ones on which political opposition to the two superpowers can be aroused and mobilized, especially in the Third World, with China playing a leading, or at least highly vocal, role. Hence, Peking seems to have approached many of the issues involved in political terms. In some respects the Chinese, unlike leaders of the other nuclear powers, appear to assume that it is not necessary to give high priority to measures to increase strategic stability in relations among nuclear powers because they tend to play down, and may actually underestimate, the dangers.

But, as in many fields of Chinese policy, there is a gap between theory and practice, and between rhetoric and actual policy toward arms control. Despite their basically negative posture, the Chinese have in practice shown a willingness to consider certain practical and limited measures and even to get involved in a few, either tacitly or explicitly—unilaterally in some cases, but in a few through participation in international agreements.

Peking's unilateral and general pledge not to be the first to use nuclear weapons is a key element in its present policy. Although the Chinese now call for similar unilateral pledges by others, they conceivably might be prepared to consider negotiating agreements on this question. Though Peking calls for the total withdrawal of all foreign forces and bases abroad, in reality this is not the basis of present Chinese policy toward the United States, especially in Asia. Chinese support for limited nuclear-free zones indicates a willingness to endorse certain partial arms control measures. Their signing of Additional Protocol II of the Latin American Treaty of Tlatelolco was a step of some significance, for it was the first international arms control agreement drawn up after the establishment of the People's Republic that Peking has been willing to sign.

The fact that the Chinese have pursued a tacit nonproliferation policy is extremely important—consider what the consequences might have been if they had given nuclear weapons assistance to Indonesia or Egypt in the 1960s. In the United Nations General Assembly the Chinese have agreed to maintain contact with, though not yet to become a member of, a forty-nation ad hoc committee established in 1973 to examine the views of governments about the possibility of a world disarmament conference—a committee they voted in favor of when it was established. More generally, in the United Nations, they have begun gradually to play an active role in debates on arms control issues.

None of Peking's actions has involved acceptance of significant constraints limiting further development of China's own nuclear capabilities, but this is understandable, in view of China's relative nuclear weakness. And despite China's opposition to most arms control measures, its policies do not exclude the possibility of its becoming involved in bilateral agreements, arrangements, or understandings with the United States.

In striving to engage the Chinese in arms control efforts, the United States on its part should have several goals in mind. One should be to stabilize the bilateral U.S.-China nuclear relationship to minimize and if possible eliminate the danger of nuclear threats, accidents, or unauthorized firings. Beyond that, the United States should work toward more far-reaching understandings or agreements with China that will further contribute to: (1) increased regional stability, especially in nuclear relations in East Asia; (2) nonproliferation of nuclear weapons; (3) eventual elimination of the nuclear component from the strategic equation in Asia; and (4) improved overall U.S.-China relations. A dialogue between the two governments on arms control might also, by bolstering their sense of security, encourage the Chinese to adopt policies of restraint in their nuclear development, particularly of weapons capable of threatening the United States. The long-term U.S. aim should be to draw China into greater, and more constructive, involvement in broad international discussions and agreements on arms control, and eventually into ones that can contribute to strategic stability among the United States, the Soviet Union, and China.

Washington should accept China as a significant, even if still relatively weak, nuclear power. It can and should operate on the assumption that China's nuclear arsenal is useful only for defensive purposes. It should accept the idea that China will acquire a credible nuclear deterrent, and its nuclear policy toward China as well as toward the Soviet Union should be based unambiguously on the concept of deterrence; Washington's rejection of a policy of "damage denial" aimed at preventing or post-poning China's acquisition of a credible deterrent is already implied in its policy of forgoing construction of a large antiballistic missile system.

In the period immediately ahead, priority should be given to the relatively modest goal of initiating *bilateral* discussions with Peking in the arms control field. Washington should do what it can, however, to persuade Peking to associate itself in some way with as many of the existing international agreements as possible, even though there can be no great hope that Peking will soon explicitly endorse those it has op-posed. The United States should try particularly hard to persuade the Chinese to further clarify their position on the nonproliferation issue. It would be highly desirable if they were to decide to follow the French example of pledging to conform to the treaty's requirements even while continuing to avoid formal association with it. Washington should make it clear to China that U.S. policy is designed to maintain conditions that will convince Taiwan and Korea as well as Japan that it is not in their interest to acquire nuclear weapons, and it should impress on Peking the fact that China's policies will be a major factor determining whether or not this is possible.

Greater efforts should also be made by the United States, as well as other nations, to involve China actively in UN-sponsored negotiations aimed at arms control agreements, in the hope that Peking, as a partici-pant, will endorse their results. Attempts to draw China into multilateral efforts should not, however, be a substitute for, or at the expense of, U.S. efforts to initiate bilateral discussions.

To increase the chances for success, Washington must try to deter-mine the kinds of proposals that will have the greatest possibility of evok-ing Chinese interest and concentrate on them at the start. Realistically speaking, these probably cannot immediately include agreements that would limit China's ability to strengthen its own nuclear deterrent. Washington must be willing to adopt a gradual, step-by-step approach, beginning with quite small steps. It should not assume that explicit, formal agreements are the only desirable goals. Instead it should recog-nize that certain types of tacit understandings—for example, ones call-ing for parallel actions, without formal agreements—may be the best that can be hoped for at the start.

The United States cannot ignore the fact that China's Third World interests may argue against dealing directly on many issues with either superpower. A deliberate effort will have to be made to overcome this obstacle. Finally, the United States in its bilateral arms control dealings with China must take full account of the implications for, and repercussions on, their triangular relationships with the Soviet Union and with Japan. It will be essential to minimize possible adverse effects of U.S.-China interactions on each nation's relations with the Soviet Union, and to follow a policy of close, prior consultation with Japan.

The agenda of specific actions that the United States should consider taking in the period immediately ahead includes several steps. The first need, obviously, is to try to initiate a genuine U.S.-China dialogue on arms control issues, preferably on an official level, though a beginning might be made through nonofficial talks like the Pugwash meetings between U.S. and Soviet groups. One basic aim, at the start, should be simply to increase understanding of existing attitudes, assumptions, and policies, on both sides. The United States should try to stimulate a thorough discussion of the risks of nuclear instability, the dangers of proliferation, the problem of possible nuclear accidents or nonauthorized firings, the desirability of and prerequisites for stable mutual deterrence, and, in light of these problems, the potential value to both countries—as well as others—of particular arms control measures.

If a serious dialogue can be initiated, an area of action worth exploring relatively early is the problem of preventing nuclear accidents or unauthorized firings, and avoiding actions that increase such dangers. There is a need for leaders in each country to have greater knowledge of and confidence in the command and control procedures and technologies employed by the other. Each should also accept the need to avoid actions the other might consider provocative. Here the United States can take a variety of unilateral actions. It can, for example, make clear that it will avoid provocative intelligence-gathering flights over Chinese territory of aircraft or drones (but not of high-flying satellites). It could also offer, unilaterally, to provide China with data on the methods and technology used in U.S. command and control systems; the aim would be, on the one hand, to increase Chinese confidence in U.S. policies and, on the other, to provide information the Chinese can use to improve their own systems.

If a useful dialogue can be initiated, Washington should, in the not too distant future, explore the possibility of concluding specific bilateral agreements with China, including ones comparable to those it has with the Soviet Union: for example, on a "hot line" between the capitals of the two countries, for consultation in emergencies or crises; on the prevention of accidental or unauthorized firings of nuclear weapons; and on the avoidance of nuclear war, with urgent consultation if there appear to be risks of war occurring. The United States should make it clear that it would also favor agreements of this sort in due time between Peking and Moscow.

When it appears feasible, Washington should also try to discuss with Peking the possibility of a carefully defined and delimited agreement on no first use of nuclear weapons. Even though the United States has already adopted policies such as forgoing the building of a large ABM system that should have indicated it is not seeking to perpetuate a first-strike capability against China, nevertheless in view of past U.S. nuclear threats against China in the 1950s, as well as the huge dimensions of the United States' continuing nuclear superiority, China's sense of security could be significantly enhanced by a U.S. no-first-use pledge. From the U.S. point of view, an agreement of this sort would institutionalize the Chinese no-first-use pledge in the form of an international agreement and reinforce broader efforts to prevent proliferation of nuclear arms. Conceivably it could be a breakthrough that might induce Peking to consider further involvement in arms control.

American opponents of the idea of a no-first-use agreement with China may argue that it would involve a major concession on the U.S. part (that is, renunciation of the right to use nuclear threats to deter major conventional as well as nuclear action by China or its allies) for little concrete gain. In reality, however, there are virtually no foreseeable circumstances, even in the event of conflict in the East Asian region, in which the dangers, and the political, psychological, and moral costs, of first use of nuclear weapons would not outweigh the possible advantages of using them. There is no reason why such an agreement should significantly weaken the credibility of the U.S. nuclear deterrent against first use by any other nation. Hence, any concession on the U.S. part would be more theoretical than real, assuming that the United States and its allies maintain adequate conventional forces to protect their vital security interests in the region.

Opponents of an agreement of this sort may also fear it might increase the risk that China could consider large-scale conventional military action beyond its borders. The inhibitions against such action by China, however, do not depend primarily on nuclear deterrence, but rather on multiple internal and external political, economic, and military constraints, including the dangers of conventional military retaliation if it were to embark on major military adventures abroad.

In specific terms, Washington should consider discussing with Peking an agreement in which both countries would pledge no first use of nuclear weapons against the forces and territories of each other. The agreement could be made to apply to the forces and territories of their respective allies, or an agreement could be linked to other agreements on nuclear-free zones.

A no-first-use agreement would appear to be of definite value to China, but there is no guarantee that it will be interested. Peking may simply continue to insist that all nuclear powers should make unilateral pledges comparable to China's and that these should be applicable worldwide, not just regionally. (From the U.S. perspective a unilateral U.S. pledge would have far fewer advantages than one agreed upon with China, and a worldwide pledge would involve far greater problems because of its implications for the complex U.S. relationships in Europe with Western European countries and the Soviet Union.) Nevertheless, despite the uncertainty about China's reactions, the United States should actively explore whether a mutually acceptable bilateral no-first-use agreement is feasible.

The United States should also be willing to discuss with China, and other concerned nations, the possibility of establishing one or more nuclear-free zones in East Asia. Accepting the premise that first use of nuclear weapons is unacceptable, the United States should explore the feasibility of agreeing on carefully defined nuclear-free zones. To begin with it would be desirable to concentrate on the possibility of establishing such a zone in Korea, perhaps in due time including Japan as well, since Japan is already—in practice if not in theory—a nuclear-free zone by the choice of the Japanese themselves.

If any nuclear-free zone is to be workable, the understandings or agreements covering it must involve all the major powers in East Asia, and all three nuclear powers would have to agree to respect the zone. In considering any such zone, especially one in Korea, it would be desirable to link the nuclear question with other issues critical to the preservation of local peace, and to devise a set of interrelated agreements, involving both the local powers and the four major powers (including Japan), aimed at deterring conventional conflicts as well as the use of nuclear weapons.

Any effort to reach agreements on nuclear-free zones in East Asia would involve complex problems. One basic obstacle would be the Sino-Soviet conflict, which at present appears to rule out any cooperation between Peking and Moscow on such problems. Nevertheless, the value that multilateral agreements could have in reducing the risks of conflict and increasing stability in the area argues for serious examination of the possibilities and efforts to discuss them with China, as well as with the Soviet Union and Japan.

In its basic approach to all the principal conflict areas on China's periphery, the United States should persistently explore whether it is possible, eventually, for the major powers to reach agreements designed to reinforce local efforts to prevent conflicts and to enhance regional security. One objective should be to obtain recognition by all the major powers of the need not only to deal with the nuclear problem but also to exercise restraint in supplying conventional arms to the smaller nations in these areas. Such restraint might lead eventually to an actual reduction in the quantity of arms supplies to these nations, and other efforts to inhibit local arms races. It would also be desirable to work toward naval agreements among the four major powers aimed at preventing an accelerating naval arms race in East Asia.

These are all immensely complicated problems, but they are extremely important. None of them—relating to either nuclear or conventional arms control—has been given the attention they deserve. Actually, even less serious consideration has been given to possible means to control conventional weapons in East Asia than to nuclear arms control issues. In part this is because such measures can only be examined as an element in the fundamental political conflicts in these areas, which are extraordinarily complex.

Exploring the possibilities of U.S. agreements with China will inevitably have repercussions affecting both the Soviet Union and Japan. Moscow will almost certainly look with disfavor on any bilateral U.S.-China discussions or agreements relating to arms control. The United States can legitimately maintain, however, that none of the agreements would be directed against Moscow, or threatening to Soviet security, and that in any case they represent less than the United States has already been willing to do with the Soviet Union in this field. Washington can also maintain, with justification, that increased involvement of China in arms control should have results, eventually if not immediately, that are favorable to all nations concerned with security in East Asia, and that the United States genuinely favors China's accommodation in this field with the Soviet Union as well as with the United States. None of this is likely to prevent great unease in Moscow, but this should not deter Washington from pursuing policies that it believes are right and important.

Some anxiety is also likely in Tokyo about the possible implications for Japan of any U.S.-China cooperation in the arms control field. Adequate U.S. consultation with the Japanese should minimize such anxieties, however. Washington should be able to reassure Tokyo that the U.S. nuclear umbrella protecting Japan would not be weakened in any way by such measures. Many Japanese, moreover, will probably themselves conclude, in time, that increased involvement of China in arms control efforts should contribute positively to the general prospects for enhancing peace and stability in East Asia, which is a fundamental objective of Japan's policies.

On balance, the arguments in favor of starting serious efforts to engage the Chinese in arms control are far more compelling than any arguments against doing so. When it initiates such efforts, however, Washington should not expect rapid results; at best the process is likely to be very gradual. Decisions on when and how to explore specific possibilities will have to be based on difficult judgments about what is likely, at any particular time, to be most persuasive to the Chinese, as well as on careful assessments of what the broader regional repercussions may be.

IV

Relations with Other Powers

FUTURE U.S. policy toward China must take full account of the broader Asian context, since U.S.-China relations will be influenced by and will have a significant impact on most other international relationships in the region. First of all, China policy must be compatible with U.S. goals in regard to the new quadrilateral pattern of relationships among the four major powers, and policymakers in Washington must carefully consider both the opportunities and the dangers involved. They must also consider the interests of the smaller nations located in potential conflict areas around China and U.S. goals in these areas. Finally, they must also take account of American objectives in regard to broad global problems.

It is clear that even though the goal of improving its relations with China is important to U.S. interests, it cannot be regarded as the only priority U.S. objective in East Asia. In fact, it is not the most important one. For a wide variety of security, economic, and other reasons, the most important single objective of U.S. policy in the region must be the maintenance of an effective, lasting, cooperative relationship with Japan. The interests of the United States and Japan, which are both highly developed, democratic societies and have extensive common economic interests, are now intertwined to a degree that U.S. and Chinese interests cannot be in the foreseeable future. In a different way, its relations with the Soviet Union are also extremely important to the United States. The United States' global security interests require that top priority be given to preventing military conflict with the Soviet Union, and this necessitates the maintenance of a stable strategic balance between the two countries and a continuing search for means to further genuine détente. This fact must be taken fully into account in U.S. policy toward any region, and especially East Asia.

Therefore, the goal of improving U.S.-China relations, important as it is, cannot be pursued at the expense of the fundamental U.S. interests in maintaining close relations with the Japanese and avoiding military conflict with the Russians.

If the United States were to be confronted with stark choices, in which the advantages of improved relations with China had to be weighed against the likelihood of a serious deterioration of U.S.-Japanese relations or a greatly increased danger of a U.S.-Soviet conflict, Washington would have little alternative but to give improved Sino-American relations the lower priority. An effective foreign policy, however, should prevent the necessity of making such undesirable choices. Nevertheless, conflicts among various U.S. objectives will inevitably arise, often in subtle and complex forms. In shaping its Asian policy Washington will constantly have to weigh the benefits and costs of alternative policies as they affect its multiple interests and objectives in relation to many nations in the region.

In broad terms, the United States should hope that a pattern of relationships based on growing cooperation among all the nations in East Asia will gradually evolve. But that would be far too simple a basis for practical policy; it would reflect pious hope more than a sober assessment of realities in the region, where serious clashes of interest persist and real dangers of conflict still exist.

In realistic terms, Washington can and should base its East Asian policy on the premise that it is both possible and desirable to maintain, and gradually stabilize, a new equilibrium among the four major powers in the region, with relationships affecting the smaller powers adjusted to fit the new situation. This not only reflects the realities of trends in recent years; it holds out more hope for preserving peace in the region than any alternative approach would. The concept of containment which shaped U.S. policy for so many years is no longer valid, although maintaining some sort of military balance still is. The Nixon Doctrine does not now provide an adequate, broad framework for policy. And a major U.S. disengagement from East Asia would sacrifice important U.S. interests and probably increase the danger of conflict among China, the Soviet Union, and Japan.

Although the broad trend toward a new equilibrium in which the United States, China, the Soviet Union, and Japan all play important though different roles, has created many uncertainties, problems, and dangers, the present situation is nevertheless preferable to that in the

1960s when Washington was locked in hostile confrontation with Peking and was engaged in actual war in Vietnam. Today, the dangers of large-scale military conflicts involving the major powers, though by no means eliminated, appear to have diminished because of the constraints that the four-power relationship imposes on all, and the likelihood that if any of the four were to embark on dangerously threatening policies, the other three would oppose it, in parallel if not in cooperation.

If the United States accepts the proposition that a more stable four-power equilibrium is a desirable goal to work toward in East Asia, it must also accept a number of corollaries. It must recognize that all four of the big powers—China and the Soviet Union as well as the United States and Japan—will play important regional roles; it is neither feasible nor desirable to try to totally exclude any of them from significant roles. The United States should continue to oppose big-power policies that pose military threats to others, but it should not automatically oppose increased economic and political participation in regional affairs on the part of any of the four powers involved.

The idea of a four-power equilibrium implies that no single power (or combination of powers) should be permitted, or is likely, to establish hegemony in the region—or even the kind of predominance that the United States enjoyed in much of East Asia in the two decades following World War II. Washington must accept that this applies to itself as well as to others; it must now view itself not as the predominant power in the region but rather as one of four major powers all of whom are principal actors.

However, the United States should continue to play an active and influential role in the region, economically, politically, and in preserving a military balance. Today, partly as a result of U.S. failures in the Indochina states, American influence has declined, but the United States nevertheless continues to play extremely important regional roles which can and should be sustained. Any U.S. withdrawal from the area, or for that matter any dramatic further decline in American influence, could alter the situation fundamentally. The consequences would doubtless tend to destabilize the existing balance. It could cause major big-power realignments and lead to a very different and less stable pattern of relationships, from which the United States would be largely excluded.

The concept of a four-power equilibrium, of the kind that has been evolving in East Asia, does not imply that all of the powers will or should have identical roles or influence, or that there will be equilateral relations among all of them. In fact, in its present form, the equilibrium *depends* on the continuation of a close relationship between the United States and a lightly armed, nonnuclear Japan, as well as on the absence of either close collaboration between Peking and Moscow or open Sino-Soviet military conflict. Any far-reaching realignment of the big powers or other radical changes in their relationships could be destabilizing. A basic aim of U.S. policy, therefore, should be to minimize the possibility of major realignments occurring.

As the new equilibrium has evolved, the importance of political and economic factors in regional relationships has clearly increased, relatively at least, while the salience of military factors has declined. United States policy must reflect this fact, which means that, while the United States can and should reduce its military role in the region, it must continue active efforts to promote its political and economic interests in, and expand its nonmilitary contributions to, the region.

However, it would be an error to conclude that military-security factors are no longer important, or that the United States can consider totally withdrawing its military forces from the region. More than in many other regions, security and the maintenance of a balance of power continue to be priority concerns of virtually all the nations involved in East Asia. Not only are both Peking and Moscow still obsessive about the military-security factors that affect their positions and relationships, most of the smaller nations in East Asia continue to be acutely sensitive to potential threats to their security. Most of them are trying to develop balanced relationships with all four of the major powers. Increasingly they rest their hopes for peace on the prospect that a new equilibrium among the major powers will impose restraints on all of them in their dealings with the smaller nations, and they increasingly recognize that security problems must now be viewed in broad political and economic terms, not simply as a military problem.

Nevertheless, regional stability will still require the maintenance of a viable military balance, or sense of balance, or at least a belief that no dangerous military imbalance is likely soon to develop. For both political and military reasons, therefore, the United States should continue to maintain a regional military presence that is significant, even if smaller than in the past. The need for this is attested to by the fact that not only Japan and most of the smaller noncommunist nations in the area, but China as well, favor a continued U.S. military role. The size and location of existing American forces and bases within the region will doubtless have to be further adjusted, and perhaps reduced, but the United States must still help to prevent dangerous imbalances.

If maintaining an equilibrium and working to make it more stable are accepted as a primary purpose of U.S. policy toward East Asia, this broad aim must shape policies toward particular countries and problem areas. The United States must attempt, first of all, to forestall dangerous new frictions and conflicts among *any* of the four major powers that could be seriously destabilizing. It must also actively search for new ways—if possible involving increased cooperation among the major powers—to defuse potential conflicts among the smaller nations, especially conflicts that could lead to big-power involvement. Increased reliance will have to be placed on political strategies to achieve these goals. The U.S. military role will inevitably be more limited, and there is little possibility that use of U.S. ground forces will be considered, except where vital American security interests are involved, as in Northeast Asia. However, the new constraints on the use of military forces will not put the United States in a unique position. Constraints on use of military power by all the other major powers will be at least as great as those on the United States.

In positive terms, U.S. policy should place increased emphasis on the need to expand normal, peaceful, political, economic, and other relationships with and among all countries in the region, encouraging greater regional and subregional cooperation, supporting developmental programs that emphasize equity within and among East Asian nations, and devising cooperative approaches to the problems created by growing economic interdependence. This demands more effective efforts to expand trade, improve investment practices, assure access to markets, achieve fair prices, and guarantee the availability of needed energy, food, and other basic commodities to all countries in the region.

Regional relationships will continue to undergo changes in the years immediately ahead. Whether the transitional period results in a more stable equilibrium or new tension and conflict will depend in considerable part on how successful the United States is in pursuing its goals, including the goal of improving relations with China. It will obviously also depend very much on the policies of the other major nations as well.

Interactions with the Soviet Union

There is no way in which the United States itself can determine the policies that the other major powers in East Asia will pursue toward each other, but U.S. policy will be an important factor influencing the judgments made by leaders in these countries about the policies they believe to be in their interest. Americans should be clear in their own minds, therefore, what they believe to be desirable.

In trying to handle the complex problems created by the new triangular relationship among the United States, the Soviet Union, and China, Washington should now accept certain basic premises about relations between Peking and Moscow from the perspective of U.S. interests. One is that any far-reaching rapprochement, which might lead to renewed, close Chinese-Russian cooperation in pursuing policies hostile to the United States, would be extremely adverse to U.S. interests. A second, however, should be that any large-scale Sino-Soviet military conflict would be equally undesirable.

A far-reaching Sino-Soviet rapprochement would pose new threats to many specific U.S. interests and would stimulate renewed bipolarization in all of East Asia, threatening the four-power relationships that have emerged in recent years. It could have very undesirable effects on the United States' closest allies; it might well, for example, result in increased pressures for major remilitarization in Japan. However, the depth of Chinese-Russian hostility in recent years makes a far-reaching rapprochement seem unlikely. It would become a real possibility only if there were basic changes in other relationships, such as a serious deterioration of U.S.-China relations (particularly if Chinese fears of an acute U.S. threat were revived). Further steps to consolidate Sino-American relations should minimize this possibility.

At the other extreme, a Sino-Soviet military conflict would also be highly undesirable, even if the United States were able to avoid direct involvement in it. Sino-Soviet war would threaten to destabilize the East Asian region as a whole at least as much as rapprochement would. In fact, any significant intensification of Sino-Soviet tensions, even short of war, would raise fears throughout the region and set back the quest for a more stable equilibrium.

To help minimize these dangers, the United States should continue to pursue balanced policies aimed at improving relations with both Peking and Moscow, and it should strongly urge restraint on both. Not only should Washington oppose any Soviet military pressures or threats directed against China, it should equally oppose belligerent or provocative Chinese policies (even assuming they are defensively motivated) that are directed against the Soviet Union. While not in any way implying that the United States might become directly involved if a Sino-Soviet military conflict should occur, Washington should make clear to both sides that the costs would be immense to all concerned, and in particular to the country that bore the greatest responsibility for precipitating a military conflict. In fact, a Sino-Soviet war could end all immediate hopes for real détente, globally as well as regionally.

Even though U.S. interests require opposition to any far-reaching Peking-Moscow rapprochement, Americans should not assume, as many do today, that a continuation of Sino-Soviet tensions at their present level is desirable. Intensely hostile relations between big powers involve too many risks and potential costs. The United States should therefore positively encourage a gradual reduction in Sino-Soviet tensions, through a step-by-step process of limited détente, comparable to that Washington itself is now striving to achieve with both Peking and Moscow.

Limited Sino-Soviet détente, and the resulting changes in the triangular pattern of Sino-American-Soviet relations, would not necessarily produce another situation of extreme imbalance; it might instead create a new triangular pattern in which the three bilateral relationships are more symmetrical than at present. There is little reason to believe that either Peking or Moscow would like to return to the pattern of confrontation and conflict with the United States characteristic of the 1950s and 1960s.

The largest risk is that Moscow might see opportunities to shift its forces and apply greater pressures on Europe. But this danger should not be exaggerated. Limited détente between China and the Soviet Union would not eliminate the two countries' mutual fears. It is possible that if Peking's security concerns vis-à-vis Moscow are reduced, it may see less need than at present to compromise in dealing with the United States. If U.S.-China relations were stalemated and Peking decided to focus prime attention once more on unresolved problems, it might, for example, be tempted to apply strong pressures again on Washington to solve the Taiwan problem. Even under such circumstances, however, it seems likely that Peking would continue to be constrained by factors and considerations that did not exist in the 1950s, when it last attempted to induce changes in U.S. policy by exerting military pressure. The legacy of a decade and a half of Sino-Soviet debate and tension makes it highly unlikely that Peking's concern about possible future dangers to the north will totally disappear. And pragmatic Chinese leaders are not likely to ignore the potential value, in security terms, of maintaining a significant American connection, even if the need seems less pressing than during recent years. Moreover, Chinese leaders would still have to consider carefully the risks and costs of actions that could lead to a serious deterioration of Sino-American relations. The Chinese are strongly motivated by a desire to avoid excessive dependency on any outside power and wish to achieve maximum freedom of action in dealing with both Moscow and Washington; this would be difficult to achieve if their relations with the United States became intensively hostile again. These factors would tend to constrain Peking even if its relations with Washington remained limited.

If broader economic and other links of mutual benefit can be developed between China and the United States, giving both sides a positive stake in good relations, the Chinese will also have to take the cost of sacrificing them into account in determining their policies. This will not eliminate the dangers of renewed Sino-American conflict. That will depend on the ability of both Peking and Washington to deal with many bilateral problems, to compromise on some, and to live with others that cannot be solved in the near future. But the main point here is that relations between China and the United States would not necessarily be seriously affected in adverse ways by a limited reduction in tensions between Peking and Moscow, nor would their triangular relationship with the Soviet Union necessarily be destabilized.

In fact, although a limited Sino-Soviet détente would clearly create some anxieties in the United States, as well as in other nations, and in the short run could marginally reduce the incentives for both Peking and Moscow to compromise with Washington, the long-run consequences could on balance be favorable in relation to certain basic U.S. goals. Minimizing the risks of Sino-Soviet war should contribute to stabilizing the big-power equilibrium in East Asia by reducing the dangers of one of the most calamitous conflicts that could occur. More broadly, limited Sino-Soviet détente—assuming, as one can, that it does not lead to restoration of a close alliance—could eventually open up new possibilities for détente regionally. For example, if it reduces the intensity of Sino-Soviet competition in Korea and Southeast Asia, it would moderate one of the most destabilizing factors in both areas. In time, it might enhance the prospects for four-power cooperation designed to prevent local conflicts in these areas, which should be a high-priority goal in Washington's policy.

While accepting the virtual certainty of continuing big-power competition in both Northeast and Southeast Asia, Washington should do what it can to reduce the dangers of conflict among all the powers involved, including China and the Soviet Union, and it should strive to obtain general acceptance, eventually, that it is in the long-run interest of all to work to stabilize these areas. The present Sino-Soviet conflict blocks any possibilities of significant four-power cooperation concerning these areas; a limited Sino-Soviet détente would not automatically make such cooperation possible, but it would at least remove a basic barrier that exists today.

To pursue a balanced policy toward China and the Soviet Union, the United States must avoid the temptation to manipulate the Sino-Soviet conflict crudely for short-term gains, although it can legitimately use whatever leverage it possesses to press for more meaningful détente. It must make clear that it will oppose attempts by either Peking or Moscow to use Washington against the other, which may not be easy to do. At present both Moscow and Peking *are* trying to manipulate Washington and use their ties with it to harm the interests of the other. Each would like to see U.S. relations with the other deteriorate rather than improve; and each regards U.S. dealings with the other as damaging to its own interests.

This situation poses many dilemmas for Washington, since steps to improve relations with either inevitably risk damaging relations with the other. This is true, for example, of U.S. steps toward arms control with the Soviet Union, and it will be true of U.S. efforts to develop negotiations on arms control with China, if these can be initiated. Washington cannot, however, allow the built-in problems to immobilize its policy and prevent it from trying to improve relationships with both Communist powers.

Because U.S. ties with Peking are still far less extensive than those with Moscow, and because Peking is clearly the weakest power in the military equation, a balanced policy will require more far-reaching changes in U.S. relations with China than with Russia; Moscow will doubtless view this as a pro-Peking tilt. Peking will also continue to view any U.S.-Soviet cooperation with suspicion. In this situation, the only sensible approach for the United States is to judge each possible move toward either country on its own merits, be extremely sensitive to the potential effects of any move on the triangular relationships, and try to avoid actions that could obviously have seriously destabilizing effects. Applying these principles will never be easy, and judgments about the likely consequences of particular moves will have to be made on the basis of the specific situation that exists when decisions must be made. Whatever actions Washington takes, especially on problems of direct relevance to military security which will affect the triangular relationship, it should make a conscious effort to convince both Peking and Moscow that the United States does not desire to damage either's legitimate interests, has no intention of aligning with one side versus the other, and is not pursuing a manipulative balance-of-power policy, but rather that it is committed to achieving multilateral détente and increased regional stability.

Interactions with Japan

Differences over China policy caused major strains in U.S.-Japan relations in the 1950s and 1960s, but since 1972 this situation has fundamentally changed. Today, both Washington and Tokyo are attempting, by similar means and in parallel, to improve relations with Peking, and Moscow as well. Moreover, the Chinese have explicitly endorsed the present U.S.-Japan relationship, including the security treaty, as a counterweight to Soviet influence.

The trend toward improved Sino-Japanese relations is clearly desirable from the U.S. point of view, because it not only reduces the potential danger of Peking-Tokyo conflict but also because it contributes to the stabilization of the four-power equilibrium in East Asia. Improved Sino-Japanese relations have helped, rather than hindered, the improvement of U.S.-China ties, and the reverse is true as well.

Even though the Japanese have since 1972 gone further than the Americans in expanding ties with China, their relations with Peking remain limited, especially in comparison to Japanese-American ties. Unless Tokyo were to begin to collaborate with Peking far more extensively, and in ways that damage U.S.-Japan relations—which does not seem likely in the period immediately ahead—there is no reason for Washington to view closer Sino-Japanese relations with concern. Instead, it should endorse the current trend as a constructive one, since peace between China and Japan is a prerequisite for stability in the entire region. Washington cannot, in any case, view Japan simply as a Western-type, modernized, industrial country allied to the United States; the Japanese still feel very much a part of Asia, and their Asian relationships are extremely important to them.

Tokyo faces complicated problems, however, in its dealings with China and the Soviet Union, similar to but even more acute than those that Washington confronts. Moreover, future changes in Chinese or Soviet policy could create new strains in U.S.-Japanese relations. United States policy must take account of these possibilities. While Washington should strive to minimize frictions in all multilateral relationships in the region, it must work against any trends that could threaten its ties with Japan, which now constitute one of the foundations of regional stability.

While one cannot exclude the possibility that future Japanese leaders could decide to lean toward China, politically and economically, in ways that might weaken or even undermine the U.S.-Japan relationship, this seems highly unlikely as long as Japan's positive stake in its U.S. relationship remains large. American and Japanese economic and other interests are so extensively linked today that even leaders of the major Japanese opposition groups, such as the Socialist party, who have argued for much closer Sino-Japanese ties as well as for changes in U.S.-Japan security relations, acknowledge that Japan must continue to maintain close and friendly relations with the United States. Few Japanese see any realistic possibility of China becoming a real substitute for the United States, in relation to Japan's economic and security interests. The Chinese on their part give no evidence of any desire to expand their Japanese relations in an unlimited fashion; their determination to control and restrict contacts with all foreign nations, and to avoid a dependence on any, applies to Japan as well as other nations. The chances of this situation changing will be small so long as Washington continues its commitment to maintaining close ties with Japan.

If future changes in Chinese policy were to cause new tensions to grow between either Peking and Washington, or Peking and Tokyo, this could obviously create new and potentially serious strains in U.S.-Japan relations (the implications of such possibilities are discussed below). But today this is not a major problem.

Some of the most difficult foreign policy problems facing Japan at the moment derive from the complexities of its triangular relationship with Peking and Moscow. Japan, like the United States, clearly hopes for a genuinely stable big-power equilibrium in East Asia. Toward this end it is attempting, through its policy of so-called equidistance, to improve relations with both China and the Soviet Union. But both Peking and Moscow are pursuing highly manipulative policies toward Tokyo. Each is trying by pressure and inducement to increase its own ties with Japan while at the same time exacerbating Japan's problems in relations with its adversary. In theory Japan should be able to balance the two, remain invulnerable to pressures from either, and extract concessions from both—as the United States seems to some extent to do in its relations with the two Communist powers. Instead, Japan's leaders today feel vulnerable to, and harassed by, competing Chinese and Soviet pressures, and often it is Tokyo rather than Peking or Moscow that feels compelled to consider major concessions.

Although it would be unwise for Washington to intervene directly in disputes between Tokyo and either Moscow or Peking, the United States should as a close ally of Japan's give political support to those Japanese positions that are reasonable in its view and oppose manipulative political pressures exerted by either of the Communist powers. It would be reasonable, for example, for Americans publicly to favor a solution of the northern islands dispute between Tokyo and Moscow that would involve Soviet concessions to Japanese nationalist sentiment; on this issue Americans can speak with considerable moral authority, having resolved a comparable legacy from World War II in returning Okinawa to Japan. Americans should favor reasonable compromise of conflicting Chinese and Japanese views and claims regarding disputed islands and national rights in the oceans between their two countries, which would require an accommodating attitude on Peking's part. Decisions on whether or not Washington should officially take public positions on such issues, and if so when and how, should be based in part on whether Tokyo desires it to do so, and in part on U.S. judgments about the likely political effects. But Washington should in any case try to bolster the confidence of Japanese leaders in their own ability to resist unreasonable demands by Peking or Moscow. The United States should hope that Japan can eventually conclude the long-discussed peace treaties with both China and the Soviet Union, but only on terms Tokyo believes reasonable and not because of relentless pressures from Peking and Moscow.

More generally, and positively, Washington should strive to coordinate its policies with Tokyo and to evolve parallel, and when possible cooperative or joint, initiatives to expand contacts and improve relations with both Peking and Moscow. Cooperation between American and Japanese private business enterprises would be desirable, for example, in exploring major developmental possibilities in both China and Siberia. In regard to the development of oil and other energy resources in either the Soviet Union or China, the possibility of joint projects involving U.S. and

Japanese technology and capital should be explored. Washington and Tokyo should agree, however, that neither will participate in certain types of projects—such as the building of a second trans-Siberian railway—that Peking would clearly regard as hostile to its interests since it would increase the Soviet Union's military advantages over China. Even if areas of cooperation between Japan and the United States can be expanded, it is inevitable that there will be competition in their dealings with China and the Soviet Union, but such competition can be accepted with equanimity.

In its dealing with China, Washington should applaud Peking's current recognition of Japan's need for a sense of security and its acceptance of the U.S.-Japan security treaty. With the full knowledge of the Japanese, American leaders should attempt to reach a genuine understanding with Peking's leaders that one important aim of both countries should be to ensure that Japan will feel no need to develop nuclear weapons in the future. Both should agree that preservation of a lightly armed Japan is in the interests of all nations in East Asia, and that all the other major powers should consciously avoid policies or actions that could so seriously threaten Japan that its leaders would feel compelled to consider rearming on a large scale. The United States should attempt to persuade leaders in Peking to take this aim fully into account in all their East Asian policies, especially toward areas of potential conflict such as the Korean peninsula and Southeast Asia and the ocean areas of the region. If Washington and Peking can reach understandings on these matters, this should reinforce the constraints on both in responding to the threat of local conflicts. The United States should also attempt to impress this view on the Russians, stressing particularly the dangers of naval rivalries that could impel the Japanese to conclude that their vital ocean lifelines are threatened and that they should therefore embark on major naval rearmament themselves.

Because the triangular relationship among the United States, China, and Japan today involves relatively few immediate problems, it appears stable. But this situation could change if Chinese policies were to shift or if new local conflicts threatening to regional stability were to break out on China's periphery. The United States should discuss with China the entire range of problems and dangers that could arise in East Asia and possible ways of minimizing the dangers. With the Japanese, the Americans should go further; they should try, jointly, to anticipate the most serious problems that could arise and consult beforehand on how best to meet them in ways that would minimize strains in the U.S.-Japan relationship.

Many problems could, in theory at least, arise in the future. If, for example, future Chinese leaders were to resume hostile attacks on the treaty relationship between Japan and the United States and deliberately tried once again to split the two, they could doubtless help to reactivate political debates within Japan in ways that might create serious strains in Japanese relations with the United States. Intensified Chinese political attacks on American or Japanese economic and political involvements in South Korea might have similar results. However, even overt, crude Chinese political attacks would not necessarily strain U.S.-Japan relations in any disastrous fashion, although they might make China policy an extremely contentious issue within Japan again. In fact, the net result might be to impel government leaders in both Washington and Tokyo to reemphasize their common interests and to strengthen cooperative efforts.

A new North-South conflict in Korea would create great dangers, and pose difficult choices, for both Washington and Tokyo. One critical question would be whether, if Washington were called upon to fulfill its defense commitment to Seoul, Tokyo would allow the Americans to use Japanese bases to aid South Korea, knowing that there would be a risk that China or Russia could become involved. It seems highly likely that in such a situation Japanese leaders would decide that they had to cooperate with the United States to meet what both governments would almost certainly consider a major threat to Japan, to U.S.-Japan relations, and to the foundations of regional stability. But it is not certain.

Situations of a different type, which could strain or destabilize the triangular U.S.-China-Japan relationship, could also arise in Southeast Asia. Direct use of Chinese military force in a local conflict there could have far-reaching effects, and although this possibility is unlikely, it cannot be totally excluded. Major Chinese military action could reverse the trend toward détente between both the United States and Japan and China and compel both to reassess their views concerning the "China threat" and adjust their basic policies accordingly. The results would probably, on balance, tend to reinforce a sense of common Japanese-American interest, but they could also strain relations. If the United States were to intervene, even with large-scale military aid, in such a situation, Japanese opinion would probably be badly divided. Conceivably, as during the Vietnam war, there could be strong pressures to dissociate

Tokyo's policy from Washington's. However, in certain situations, U.S. nonintervention, or seeming American indifference to the outcome of local conflicts, could also affect Japanese-American relations adversely, raising questions in the minds of some Japanese about the U.S. willingness to defend not only American interests but those of its allies in East Asia. The low probability of direct Chinese military action in Southeast Asia in the period immediately ahead makes these contingencies unlikely, but they cannot be ignored.

It is possible that in the longer run Sino-Japanese relations in Southeast Asia could become increasingly competitive, and eventually hostile, as a result of an unrestrained growth of Japan's economic power in the region paralleled by a steady rise in China's political involvements there. Such a situation could pose difficult issues for U.S. policy toward both Peking and Tokyo and require choices that Washington would prefer to avoid. This situation is less likely to arise, however, if the United States continues to play an active economic role in Southeast Asia. If it does not, Sino-Japanese tensions in the region might grow and greatly complicate U.S. relations with both countries.

Some of the greatest uncertainties about the future of the complex triangular relationship involving the United States, Japan, and China concern Taiwan. If the United States adopts the policies outlined in chapter 2, its policies and those of Japan, toward both China and Taiwan, will be similar. Both will then have formal ties with Peking and nonofficial relations with Taiwan, and both will be operating on the premise that Peking is not likely to destabilize the situation by resuming active military pressures or threats against Taiwan. Though there are good reasons to believe that this premise will prove to be correct, one cannot exclude the possibility that future Chinese leaders might adopt a more militant and threatening posture toward Taiwan once again. This would immediately pose painful dilemmas for both Washington and Tokyo, which unquestionably could result in serious strains in U.S.-Japan relations.

The Japanese government's reaction to a danger of renewed conflict in the Taiwan area might be highly ambivalent, and Japanese public opinion would probably be divided. Some Japanese would probably regard military action in the Taiwan area as so seriously threatening to Japan's interests that Tokyo could not simply watch passively. Others, however, would probably argue that Japan should avoid involvement in any conflict over Taiwan, and should dissociate itself from the United States if it were to become involved. The dilemmas facing policymakers in Washington would be even more difficult. Some Americans would oppose any involvement in a military conflict in the area. However, if the U.S. government remained committed to an informal pledge to continue opposing change in Taiwan's status by force, it would be compelled to consider ways to provide military support, either to deter Peking from attacking Taiwan or to help defend the island in the event of attack. The crucial issue in U.S.-Japan relations that would immediately arise would be whether or not bases in Japan could be used for this purpose. Under conceivable "worst case" circumstances, differences between Washington and Tokyo over this issue could seriously threaten, and perhaps even split, the U.S.-Japan alliance. Today, both Washington and Tokyo operate on the assumption—or the hope—that this situation will not arise. The probability that it will seems low, but one cannot say that it is not within the realm of the conceivable.

This contingency may be impossible to plan for effectively before it seems imminent since trying to do so might precipitate an unnecessary political crisis in U.S.-Japan relations. If, however, such a situation were to occur, both Washington and Tokyo would have to act rapidly and determine their policies in close consultation, weighing both the short- and the long-range consequences of cooperation or noncooperation. Preservation of the U.S.-Japan alliance should be regarded as a fundamental objective in whatever decisions Washington makes.

A divergence of American and Japanese policies concerning Taiwan could also be brought on by less dramatic—and therefore more immediately plausible—circumstances. For example, Peking might, instead of adopting an overtly threatening military posture, simply decide to apply varied kinds of direct and indirect pressure, in a step-by-step, salami-slice fashion, to persuade countries with extensive economic ties to Taiwan to reduce their trade and investments. The responses of the U.S. and Japanese governments, and of private business organizations in each country, could differ significantly, with the Japanese more inclined to accommodate to Peking's wishes. If so, the overall policies of the two countries toward Taiwan could begin to diverge again, with one moving toward disengagement from the island while the other attempted to sustain existing ties. A divergence of this sort would inevitably be reflected in their broad policies toward China. The United States should attempt, therefore, to look ahead to a contingency of this sort, considering with the Japanese how their responses might be coordinated in the event that Peking's policy were to move in this direction.

Close consultation with the Japanese government on the entire range of China policy issues will be necessary in the period immediately ahead. Otherwise, it will be difficult to develop any effective and sustainable China policy. A failure on either Washington's or Tokyo's part to carry out such consultation could result in shocks comparable to the "Nixon shocks" of the early 1970s, that might be extremely costly in terms of U.S. goals in relation to both China and Japan.

Even with effective consultation, of course, identical views will not always emerge nor will close coordination of policy always result. Tokyo may at times be prepared to adjust its views to Washington's, but at other times it will have to be the other way around, and on occasion the two governments will doubtless find it necessary to agree to disagree while trying to contain their differences within reasonable limits. But if U.S. and Japanese policies toward China do diverge in major ways, neither will have favorable prospects for success.

In the years ahead, moreover, the Japanese-American dialogue on the problems in the triangular relationship with China cannot be confined, as in the past, to U.S. consultation with the ruling Liberal Democratic party. A serious effort must be made to establish effective lines of communication between Americans and the leaders of Japan's major opposition parties, through which a systematic exchange of views on China policy—in the context of broader relationships—can take place. This appears more feasible now than ever before, in part because the improvement of relations between both Washington and Tokyo and Peking has narrowed the gap between opposing views, within Japan and between Japanese and Americans. The purpose of initiating a dialogue on China policy with all important segments of Japanese political opinion should not be simply to highlight the gradual convergence of views that has already occurred; it should aim at further reducing differences and working toward a broader consensus on how to deal with the complex new problems that will inevitably be on the agenda of China policy issues for both countries in the years ahead.

In sum, a fundamental premise of U.S. policy should be that, while steadily improving relations with China, the United States must continue to maintain and strengthen its special relationship with Japan. In a basic sense, of course, the future of Japanese-American relations will be determined less by issues concerning relations with third countries than by the success the two countries have in strengthening their ties and keeping within bounds the unavoidable strains in their bilateral relations. This will require compromise on economic issues and steps to expand U.S.-Japanese cooperation in dealing with global economic problems. It will also require efforts to increase cultural and other contacts that will deepen relationships between the two countries. In addition it will necessitate mutual accommodation to maintain a viable security relationship which genuinely serves the interests of both—which among other things will require agreement on a minimal U.S. base structure that both governments can fully support.

At present the prospects for success in coping with all of these problems are reasonably good. In looking ahead, however, Americans must accept that in reality as well as in theory, Japan is now an equal, not a subordinate, partner, and realize that Tokyo will exercise increasing independence and initiative in developing its own foreign policies. The trend over time will almost certainly be toward a somewhat looser U.S.-Japan relationship, possibly paralleled by gradually expanding Sino-Japanese ties. Americans should not view such trends with alarm so long as the essentials of the existing Japanese-American economic and security relationships can be maintained, and so long as improved Sino-Japanese relations do not result from, or cause, a deterioration in either Japanese-American or Sino-American relations.

The Problem of Korea

The greatest dangers of conflict in East and Southeast Asia that could involve the major powers are those inherent in the relationships among smaller nations in the region. Because conditions in two areas on China's periphery—the Korean peninsula and Southeast Asia—remain fundamentally unstable, and because all four major powers are inevitably involved in competitive relationships in these areas, local conflicts there could pose serious dangers for the entire region. Such conflicts, especially one in Korea, could escalate and involve one or more of the major powers militarily. Even if this did not occur, they could affect the stability of the existing equilibrium very adversely. Some of the greatest uncertainties focus on the future policies of the two Communist middle powers in the region—North Korea and North Vietnam—and on how China and the Soviet Union, which today compete fiercely for political influence over both, will pursue their goals and use their influence to support or to restrain the Koreans and Vietnamese.

The aims of U.S. policy in both Northeast and Southeast Asia should
be to reduce the immediate dangers of conflict and reinforce the constraints limiting big-power military intervention if local conflict should
occur, and over the long run to promote gradual mutual accommodation
between and among all the powers in these regions. These aims must be
taken fully into account in formulating Washington's policies toward
China and the other major powers as well as toward the smaller powers
themselves.

The question of how to preserve the peace in Korea and Southeast
Asia clearly should be a major item on the agenda of future discussions
and negotiations between American and Chinese leaders. The United
States should strive persistently to achieve understandings or agreements
on means to discourage local conflicts and on positive steps that all the
major powers should take to further the cause of peace in both areas.

It would be a grievous error, obviously, to look on Northeast and
Southeast Asia simply as arenas for big-power competition, or to view
the nations in these areas primarily as pawns of one or another of the
major powers. Every nation in the region has a distinctive history and
identity. Each is moved by its own nationalist aspirations, and each is engaged in its own search for security, political unity, economic development, and national self-fulfillment. All have particular interests and goals
that differ from those of any of the major powers or their immediate
neighbors. None wishes to be a satellite of any other power. Some are
themselves major *nations*, even if they are not major *powers*. The United
States must, of course, follow individual policies toward each of these
countries that take full account of its particular attitudes, circumstances,
and goals.

It would be an equally grievous error, however, for the United States
to try to deal with the smaller nations in East Asia without reference to
the big-power relationships there. Even though the Vietnam War highlighted the limited capability of the major powers to determine the political future of smaller nations moved by powerful nationalist and ideological forces, the long-run fate of all the nations in Northeast and Southeast
Asia will depend on the pattern of relationships that exists among the
major powers and the policies these powers pursue toward them. And the
future stability of the four-power equilibrium in East Asia will depend
on trends and developments within Northeast and Southeast Asia. In
short, the security, political fate, and economic well-being of both large
and small nations in the East Asian region as a whole remain inextricably

intertwined. It is for this reason that the United States must attempt not only to develop viable relationships with each of the smaller nations involved but also to work toward concrete understandings among the major powers designed to increase the prospects for stability in both areas.

The immediate outlook for big-power understandings concerning these areas is discouraging. The continuing commitment of the Communist nations to political struggle and revolutionary change is one basic reason. The nationalist ambitions of the two Communist middle powers is another. And today a third is the bitter rivalry between Peking and Moscow for influence in these areas, which inhibits either from taking overt steps, whether cooperatively or independently, to reduce the dangers of conflict when such steps might seem to affect their competitive position adversely. Today, while both Peking and Moscow seem less concerned than formerly about U.S. or Japanese influence in these areas, each is determined to prevent the other from achieving a dominant influence, which clearly works against the goal of achieving the kind of four-power understandings that are desirable.

It is unlikely that either Peking or Moscow will soon favor cooperative solutions to the major problems in either Korea or Southeast Asia. Nevertheless, Washington and Tokyo should continue to search for such solutions. The aim should be, through coordinated, joint, or parallel actions, to encourage increased moderation, flexibility, and compromise on the part of both Peking and Moscow, and to use whatever political and economic leverage can be mustered to persuade both the North Koreans and the North Vietnamese that restraint on their part is necessary and that mutual accommodation with other nations is in their interest. The chances of success in this effort will obviously be substantially enhanced if either the Chinese or the Russians or both can be persuaded to exert their influence to this end, on Pyongyang and Hanoi, in parallel if not cooperatively.

A successful American policy toward these areas will require understandings with Tokyo on common approaches to the major problems that must be faced. It will also require new U.S. political initiatives directed toward both the Korean peninsula and the Southeast Asian area. And it will require a major effort to engage both Peking and Moscow in serious discussion of the crucial issues affecting peace in these areas.

The situation on the Korean peninsula today poses the greatest immediate danger of war in East Asia. The two Korean regimes are among the most heavily armed and bitterly hostile in the world. All four major powers regard Korea as extremely important to their security interests—China, the Soviet Union, and Japan for historical and geographical reasons, the United States because peace in Korea is basic to the security of Japan and therefore to stability in Northeast Asia, where U.S. vital interests in East Asia are most heavily involved.

Although U.S.-China détente helped to stimulate the opening of discussions between North and South Korea in 1971, no real progress has been made toward the goal of reunification and, in fact, tensions on the divided peninsula have increased since 1974. Kim Il-sung, at the helm of a disciplined and totalitarian Communist society in the North, maintains a belligerent posture toward the South and presses for a total U.S. military withdrawal and dramatic immediate steps toward North-South unification (starting with "confederation"). He adamantly opposes, in principle, any accommodation to the reality of the existing "two-Koreas" situation. Park Chung-hee, the leader of a nontotalitarian but nevertheless authoritarian and repressive regime in the South, maintains a more defensive posture and argues for cautious, limited steps to open North-South contacts in order to begin building mutual confidence. For all practical purposes, South Korea, without in any sense abandoning the goal of ultimate reunification, now espouses policies that accept the de facto division of the peninsula.

While it is unlikely that North Korea contemplates the deliberate initiation of large-scale military action against the South, it may well continue its efforts to weaken the South, isolate it, and increase pressures on it. The greatest uncertainty concerns what Kim might do if there were signs of increased political instability in the South; the North might then increase its pressures, or step up its efforts at subversion, in an effort to exploit the situation. This could provoke incidents that might lead to escalating tensions and, conceivably, to military conflict. And if large-scale military action occurred, the major powers could soon be involved. One aim of the North's recent policies, obviously, has been to obtain as strong backing as possible from China, which currently gives it the clearest political support, and the Soviet Union, which is still the major supplier of its most advanced weaponry. Recently, Pyongyang seems to have tilted in a pro-Peking direction because the Chinese have been more willing than the Russians to back its political positions. Another of North Korea's aims has been to expand contacts with Japan and to establish direct contacts with the United States in order to weaken their support for South Korea. North Korea has also worked hard to broaden its relations with other developing countries, identifying itself increasingly, as the Chinese have done, with the Third World.

The South Korean regime, in this situation, has been obsessed by the fear of an attack from the North, especially a quick military strike directed against Seoul which is located close to the North-South dividing line. While trying to maintain its vital ties to both the United States and Japan, the South Korean government has placed increasing emphasis on the need to strengthen its basis for independent defense and foreign policies. It has worked to broaden its international ties, but with only limited success; it has also tried to open contacts with Peking and Moscow, with almost no significant results, however. Internally, Park's regime has achieved striking economic successes, but in trying to strengthen its political position by suppressing all opposition groups it has created a situation in the South that is potentially dangerous.

All four of the major powers whose interests are involved in Korea have in various ways used their influence to discourage a North-South military conflict. However, neither China nor the Soviet Union has been willing to pursue policies explicitly aimed at stabilizing the existing situation. North Korea, with the political backing it has obtained by playing Peking and Moscow against each other, has been able to maintain an uncompromising stance and to reject all proposals for mutual accommodation of a sort that any genuine North-South modus vivendi will require. In 1975 Peking publicly declared for the first time that it recognized Kim's regime as the sole legitimate government in Korea, which added a new complication to the tasks of furthering North-South détente. If Kim were to take adventurist actions, which conceivably could precipitate incidents posing the danger of open conflict, he might be able to induce Peking or Moscow, or both, because of their competition against each other, to support even risky moves.

The United States in its dealing with *all* the other nations involved in Northeast Asia should insist that peace in Korea requires a stable North-South military balance. It should make clear that it will do whatever it believes is required, including maintaining American military forces on the peninsula, to ensure the maintenance of such a balance. It should be prepared to accept a modification of, or even an end to, previous UN-endorsed arrangements in Korea, including the armistice agreement, if new arrangements can be agreed upon between North and South Korea and supported by the major powers; but it should oppose scrapping the armistice unless something new takes its place.

The United States should also indicate that, if there are significant moves toward North-South détente, it will be prepared to establish contacts with the North, aimed at ultimate normalization of U.S.-North Korea relations. It should make clear, though, that such a step will be contingent on, or must be paralleled by, steps by Peking and Moscow to establish contacts aimed at normalization of relations between themselves and the South. Washington should continue to urge the seating of both Korean regimes in the United Nations, without prejudice to their future unification, despite Pyongyang's opposition (with Peking's and Moscow's support) to what it denounces as a "two-Koreas" plot.

Above all, the United States should insist that both North and South Korea must avoid policies threatening to the other, and it should work to convince all the major powers that they should use their influence actively to persuade both Korean regimes to do this. It should make clear that progress in reducing North-South tension will be a prerequisite for, not a consequence of, withdrawals of U.S. military forces on the peninsula.

Looking to the future, the United States should urge gradual steps, if North-South tensions abate, toward a balanced reduction of military forces by both Korean regimes. In addition, it should attempt, in concert with Tokyo, to persuade China and the Soviet Union of the need, ultimately, not only for general understandings designed to deter either Korean regime from initiating military conflicts, but for specific agreements to limit arms sales to both Korean regimes, to ensure continuation of an effective demilitarized zone between the North and South (perhaps manned by an international peacekeeping force), and ultimately to make Korea a nuclear-free zone, and perhaps even a "neutralized" area.

In sum, the United States should stand firm on its pledge to defend the South in the event of attack and continue to maintain at least minimal U.S. forces in Korea under existing conditions, making clear that it will not be induced to withdraw by political pressures so long as a highly unstable North-South relationship exists. At the same time it should propose changes in the situation through balanced and reciprocal moves by the two Korean regimes and the four major powers involved.

Washington should consider taking certain unilateral steps now to try to unfreeze the present situation, while making clear that compromises on the U.S. part will remain limited until the Communist powers show increased flexibility and moderation in their policies. One desirable move would be to initiate a gradual, step-by-step reduction of U.S. military forces in Korea. To make this feasible, the United States should implement a three- to five-year military aid program designed to improve South Korea's ability to defend itself without the aid of U.S. forces, at the same time reducing the level of American ground forces on the peninsula (continuing, however, to maintain U.S. air units there as long as North-South balance in air power is unequal). At the same time it should indicate that it will not support a large-scale military buildup in the South that could upset the North-South balance, and that it will do all it can to deter South Korea from acquiring nuclear arms. While indicating that some sort of U.S. military presence will remain in Korea until reasonable stability on the peninsula is achieved, it should state its willingness to withdraw *all* American military forces from Korea when there is greater stability. Washington should leave no doubt, however, that the U.S. defense commitment, as such, will be maintained until Peking and Moscow are prepared to end their defense treaties with North Korea, and until some kind of credible international agreements or understandings makes bilateral defense treaties unnecessary.

These policies, aimed at creating and maintaining a stable military balance, should be accompanied by positive political initiatives designed to stimulate new compromises. To feel out the intentions of Pyongyang, the United States should permit, and in fact encourage, nonofficial American contacts with North Korea. In doing so, it should hold out the prospect of developing more extensive economic, as well as political, relations with North Korea, but make this contingent on changes in North Korea's policies that indicate a willingness to work toward a modus vivendi with the South, and on indications from Peking and Moscow that they are willing to consider establishing contacts with the South.

Japan's willingness to pursue policies that generally parallel those of the United States will be a virtual sine qua non for success in this approach, since Tokyo is likely to have greater economic leverage than Washington in trying to persuade leaders in Pyongyang, and perhaps Peking as well, to alter their present policies. Currently, North Korea faces some serious internal economic problems, and a major balance of payments problem, which make its economic ties to Japan increasingly important to it.

Finally, in dealing with the South, the United States must try, persistently, to persuade Park to liberalize his policies and broaden his political base, since the danger of instability in the South clearly contributes to instability in North-South relations. However, Washington must accept the fact that crude threats to end U.S. support, or to intervene directly to force political reforms, might be counterproductive; the result could be to increase political instability in the South and intensify the dangers of North-South conflict rather than to foster Korean democracy. Nevertheless, for both moral reasons, dictated by American democratic values, and pragmatic ones, relating to the dangers that oppressive policies in the South create, the United States should frankly criticize acts of political repression carried out by Park's government, as well as the totalitarian policies implemented by Kim in the North. Persuasion may encourage increased political moderation and liberalization over time. However, because of the dangerous regional consequences a Korean military conflict could produce, priority must be given to the necessity of preventing an outbreak of actual war. A gradual reduction of North-South tensions should be more effective in encouraging political liberalization in the South than U.S. attempts to intervene politically to try to force political change.

The essence of the U.S. approach toward the Korean problem should be, on the one hand, to maintain its deterrent posture and refuse to make one-sided concessions in the face of political pressures exerted by Pyongyang, with Peking's or Moscow's backing, but, on the other, to show a willingness to be flexible and initiate a step-by-step process of mutual compromise and accommodation involving the major powers as well as the two Korean regimes. The unswerving objective should be a North-South modus vivendi buttressed by agreements among the four major powers, designed to stabilize the situation on the peninsula. The United States should not challenge, and in fact should support, the ultimate goal of Korean reunification, to which both Korean regimes are strongly committed. It should insist, however, that the process of mutual accommodation today must be based on the realities of the de facto division of the peninsula.

Passive acceptance by the United States of the tense situation in Korea would involve too many dangers to be acceptable. Hence, Washington should take the initiative in pressing for compromises. Since balanced, reciprocal moves by all the nations concerned are required, however, until a process of genuine détente occurs, the United States should oppose all moves designed to undercut either South Korea's position or its own.

The Korean problem clearly is highly relevant to U.S.-China relations. The goal of achieving a stable equilibrium in East Asia will be endangered so long as Korea remains a tense area of confrontation, and U.S.-China détente is likely to be undermined if any major military conflict occurs there. Current Chinese policy and, to a lesser extent, Soviet policy as well, work against steps toward genuine political compromise in Korea and therefore help perpetuate the dangerous situation. Even if Peking opposes military conflict in Korea, as it probably does, China's strong public support has helped Kim Il-sung to maintain an uncompromising political stance, symbolized by his demands for an end to the UN Command, a total withdrawal of U.S. forces, impractical immediate moves toward North-South confederation, and the seating of only one Korean regime, his own, in the United Nations.

In many respects Peking seems to have tried to have its cake and eat it too. While it indicates that it wishes the United States to maintain a significant military presence in East Asia to counterbalance Soviet power, it nevertheless, in a contradictory fashion, endorses North Korea's demand that the United States withdraw all of its forces from Korea. Peking's determination to outdo Moscow in the contest for influence in Pyongyang explains this contradiction. However, Chinese leaders may also assume that, whatever Peking and Pyongyang do, Washington is not likely to suddenly withdraw all its forces. Consequently, they may think that they can make political capital by publicly denouncing the continuing U.S. military presence in Korea, without risking the consequences that a withdrawal might produce.

The United States should not passively accept the contradiction in Peking's positions. It should insist on discussing all aspects of the Korean situation with the Chinese and try persistently to impress upon them that, whatever short-term advantages they may gain from their present policies, the dangers inherent in the situation are too great to justify them. It should make clear that, in the American view, because détente in Korea is a prerequisite for stable peace in the whole region, it is inevitably linked to the future of U.S.-China détente. Washington can legitimately indicate that Peking's policy toward Korea is one of the factors it considers in judging China's overall intentions with respect to détente. It should emphasize that trends in Korea, whether toward compromise or intensified confrontation, will unavoidably affect U.S.-China relations, for better or for worse.

It would obviously not be realistic for the United States to ignore the political problems, especially those deriving from the Sino-Soviet conflict, that now make it difficult for Peking to modify its positions.

Moreover, Washington cannot assume that even if China shows greater flexibility, Peking can necessarily persuade Pyongyang to be more compromising. So long as the Sino-Soviet dispute continues at its present level of intensity, Kim Il-sung can turn to Moscow for backing if Peking's support weakens. Nevertheless, it is imperative to try to persuade Peking, as well as Moscow, and eventually Pyongyang, that mutual compromise is a necessity and that steps must be taken in that direction if broader trends toward détente are to be sustained.

At present there may be a greater possibility of convincing the Russians than the Chinese that this is the case. If Moscow were to show signs of much greater flexibility than Peking in regard to Korea, the United States should attempt to develop whatever cooperative or parallel policies seem possible on the issues involved, no matter how much Peking might disapprove. Washington should, of course, be prepared to do the same with Peking if it were to show the greater flexibility.

The ultimate aim must be to reach four-power understandings on how best to encourage North-South détente. If a four-power meeting seems to be a realistic possibility, the United States should press for one. However, such a meeting will probably not be feasible until the Sino-Soviet conflict moderates enough for the leaders in Peking and Moscow to be willing to sit down together to discuss major international issues. In the meantime, Washington, in cooperation with Tokyo, must try to persuade all of the Communist powers that their present policies increase the dangers of military conflict and that the only realistic path toward peace, stability, and eventual reunification in Korea is the path of genuine détente.

The Problem of Southeast Asia

In comparison with Korea, Southeast Asia today is more complex and fluid but it is less vital in security terms to U.S. interests, and less immediately dangerous to regional stability. It nevertheless poses numerous problems that the United States cannot ignore. The failure of Washington's Vietnam policy, the collapse of all the noncommunist regimes in the Indochina area, and the rise of Vietnam as a strong new Asian middle power, paralleling broader changes in big-power relations throughout East Asia have fundamentally altered the situation. The need for a new U.S. approach to the area is clear, and in redefining its policies toward

Southeast Asia the United States must take full account of the linkages between its goals and policies toward the local area and its relations with the other major powers, particularly China.

For two basic reasons Southeast Asia *today* should not be considered *vital* to U.S. *security* interests in the sense that Korea is. First, and most important, the area is not one where local military conflicts would pose immediate and direct threats to the security of a major power allied to the United States, and therefore to fundamental U.S. security interests. Second, in Southeast Asia today, even though all the major powers have important interests, none has a security stake equal to its stake in Korea, and none currently sees it as an area of overriding immediate danger to its basic security interests. Both China and the United States did appear to view it this way only a short while ago, and Peking still fears a Soviet threat there; moreover, both could alter their views in the future. But today their sense of threat is not acute. Southeast Asia remains a potentially volatile area, however, and the major powers—especially China and the Soviet Union—still fear the consequences if it should eventually come under the hegemony of an adversary. Nevertheless, the dangers of big-power military intervention resulting from local conflicts are clearly less today than in the 1950s and 1960s.

It took years of costly fighting in Vietnam for the United States to conclude that its *vital security* interests are really not at stake in Southeast Asia. This conclusion has led to a new American consensus that the United States should avoid, under foreseeable circumstances, the direct use of American ground forces in the area and should cut back the American military presence there.

Recent trends have also, however, raised doubts in many Americans' minds about whether the United States now has any significant interests in Southeast Asia. A sober assessment of the situation indicates that it clearly does. It has a large and growing economic interest in the region. Enjoying friendly ties with most of the noncommunist nations in the area, it also has a strong political interest in the ability of all these countries to survive, develop peacefully, and participate constructively in world affairs. One country in the area, Indonesia, is one of the world's major nations, in size, population, and economic potential, even though it is still underdeveloped. Two, Thailand and the Philippines, are countries with which the United States has long had close special ties. All of Southeast Asia is rich in natural resources. Furthermore, the area sits astride one of the major transportation crossroads of the world, and con-

tinued access to and transit rights through any region of this sort, anywhere in the world, should be an important U.S. objective.

Moreover, Southeast Asia cannot be viewed in isolation. Developments there will inevitably have an effect on other nations and areas
where the United States has important interests, including not only
Japan but Australia, New Zealand, and South Asia. Trends in Southeast Asia will significantly influence the stability of the new four-power
relationship in East Asia, just as the policies of the major powers will
inevitably continue to influence the evolving situation within Southeast
Asia. The United States therefore cannot be indifferent to the fate of
Southeast Asia.

Clearly, however, the new situation requires a new approach in U.S.
policies, which must be based on a realistic assessment of current trends
and problems in the area. In the wake of the U.S. withdrawal from Indochina, the prevailing mood in the region is uncertainty. There is universal recognition that a new configuration of power has emerged, but it
is impossible to know what the consequences will be.

Vietnam, under a disciplined, ambitious, Communist regime, which
possesses large stocks of captured U.S. military material as well as
Soviet and Chinese arms and equipment, has emerged as the strongest
nation in Southeast Asia in military terms. But a new kind of international competition has been introduced in the area, now that the U.S.-
China confrontation has ended and Peking and Moscow are adversaries.
China's political influence has grown substantially, as it has broadened
its diplomatic ties with the noncommunist nations. It continues, however, not only to support the Indochinese Communist states but also to
give political encouragement to several revolutionary movements in the
area, and this aspect of its policy continues to pose potential threats to
stability. The influence of the United States has obviously declined, but
it nevertheless continues to play very important political and economic
roles and still is the only external power that maintains mobile naval and
air forces in the area, albeit smaller ones than previously.

The newest element in the picture is the steady increase in both Soviet
and Japanese activities. The Russians are trying hard to expand their ties
and influence throughout the area, competing everywhere against Chinese influence. Politically and economically, they have in some respects
adopted a deliberately conservative posture, in opposition to China's
continuing though muted verbal support for revolution. However, they
may well be tempted to expand their naval activity and increase their

military aid in the area, in which case they could play an extremely disruptive and destabilizing role. Japan has emerged as the strongest economic power in the region, and its political influence, though still relatively limited, is clearly growing. Most Southeast Asians are highly ambivalent about Japan's new role, however, for they desire its trade and aid, but fear Tokyo's economic dominance. Japan's primary interests in the area are trade and investment, but its need for oil from the Middle East also gives it a vital security interest in transit rights.

The most destabilizing factors in Southeast Asia at present are the uncertainty about the future relationships among, and policies of, the newly victorious Communist regimes in Indochina and the anxiety about the possible consequences of Sino-Soviet competition for influence. The competition between the Communist powers to influence Vietnam has escalated since Hanoi's victory over South Vietnam and the U.S. withdrawal from Indochina in early 1975. The Vietnamese, who clearly do not wish to be subordinate to either the Russians or the Chinese, are trying to maintain good relations with both while pursuing their own goals. Recently, however, they appear to have tilted in a pro-Soviet direction. Historically, the Vietnamese have feared China, and they may feel that closer ties with the Soviet Union will help to counterbalance and check China's influence in Southeast Asia. In any case, Peking-Hanoi relations have recently shown strains as a result.

In pursuing their own goals, the North Vietnamese have already unified Vietnam, and they seem determined to extend their influence throughout the entire Indochina area and possibly beyond. Peking and Moscow also appear determined to increase their political influence in Laos and Cambodia, and neither seems prepared to acquiesce to the idea of Vietnamese hegemony in Indochina, though each would prefer to see Vietnamese influence predominate over that of its competitor. In Cambodia, which has undergone a far-reaching internal upheaval, Chinese influence is clearly ascendant at present. In Laos the Russians have steadily increased their direct involvements and appear to have expanded their influence, probably partly at the expense of the Chinese.

The noncommunist nations in Southeast Asia have watched all these developments with concern, uncertain about the impact of the U.S. military withdrawal, the intentions of Vietnam, and the consequences of the Sino-Soviet rivalry. All have felt compelled to adjust their policies, and the general trend has been toward limited accommodation with the Communist powers and the adoption of new policies aimed at more

balanced relations with all of the major powers. Today, all noncommunist Southeast Asian nations appear to accept the necessity to avoid
dependence on any single external power and to rely instead on a
combination of self-reliance, regional cooperation, and relations with
several major powers.

In their domestic situation, the noncommunist nations vary greatly.
In the 1960s, most of them made progress in promoting economic
growth, although the social problems accompanying development were
often tremendous and in some countries social inequities increased.
Today, in part because of social problems, there are few stable political
regimes in the area, and the general trend has been toward military
rule and increased authoritarianism. Virtually every noncommunist
nation in the area, moreover, continues to face a basic problem of coping
with armed dissidents, more often than not guerrillas to whom the Communist nations—especially China and Vietnam—give moral support and
in some cases limited material support.

Yet, despite their problems, the majority of the noncommunist Southeast Asian nations have strong assets that strengthen their prospects for
survival, viability, and development. Nationalism is a powerful force in
most of them; and it reinforces a natural determination to oppose both
internal and external threats to their national survival and integrity and
provides a basis for doing so. Most of them are relatively well endowed
with natural resources, which eases their economic problems. In none
of them, at present, are Communist or other dissident movements strong
enough to threaten the survival of the existing regime. A fundamental
reason is that nowhere in Southeast Asia outside of Indochina have the
Communists captured control of the main force of local nationalism.
The problems that guerrilla movements could pose would obviously
increase if China or Vietnam (or the Soviet Union) decided to increase material support to them; but this would not be easy to do successfully, and it could provoke a strong nationalist counteraction.
Even though there is no immediate prospect for genuine stability
within most Southeast Asian nations, there seems to be no imminent
danger of their succumbing in domino fashion to internal Communist
takeovers. Moreover, although most of the noncommunist nations will
almost certainly accommodate to some degree to Vietnam, China, and
the Soviet Union, they seem very unlikely to become closely aligned
with any one of them or to establish ties that require the severance of

their important links with the United States and Japan. The effect in most Southeast Asian nations of the new multipolarity of power relationships, in sum, is likely to be to encourage self-reliance in dealing with internal problems and increased flexibility in dealing with all external powers.

Recent trends also seem likely to encourage more serious attempts to organize regional cooperation. The efforts to develop cooperative organizations that have been under way for many years have progressed, but only slowly, and to date the results have been limited. The Association for Southeast Asian Nations (ASEAN), however, has developed into a fairly significant regional organization, politically and economically. This group, composed of Indonesia, Malaysia, Singapore, Thailand, and the Philippines, could become increasingly important in the years ahead. Leaders of ASEAN have called for "neutralization" of Southeast Asia, through the creation of a "zone of peace and neutrality." Even though the concept is ill-defined, it symbolizes a growing desire in Southeast Asia to check big-power intervention and promote regional self-reliance.

The goals of increased regional cooperation and neutralization clearly have widespread support among Southeast Asian nations, but neither will be easily achieved. Even among the noncommunist nations, numerous conflicts of interest persist, and there are deep divisions between them and the Communist states in the Indochina area. One key question is whether or not these divisions can gradually be bridged. A number of governments have begun tentative efforts to see whether normal relations with the Communist Indochinese states are possible, but it is too early to judge what the results will be.

In the immediate future, it seems likely that most of the nations of Southeast Asia will operate as members either of a loose group of noncommunist nations, with ASEAN as its core and Indonesia its strongest member, or of another consisting of Communist states in the Indochina area, with Vietnam playing the leading role. The prospect is slim, even under the most favorable circumstances, that these will soon merge so that regional cooperation, including all nations in the area, can develop. It is conceivable, though, that diplomatic ties, trade, and other contacts can bridge the ideological and political barriers that separate these groups, thereby reducing tensions and fears and encouraging mutual accommodation, and perhaps leading to limited cooperation.

It is also possible, however, that if efforts to bridge the gap between the two groups of nations fail, there could be a crystallization of two blocs, with minimal links, that face each other in hostile confrontation.

Because the new political situation in Southeast Asia is so complex, there are more questions than answers about its future. Even though many are unanswerable, U.S. policy must take all the questions into account. Will the Indochina states gradually come under the central control of one power, or will there be a delicate balance among Hanoi, Peking, and Moscow in the area? Will Hanoi be heavily preoccupied with problems of internal consolidation, or will it turn its attention increasingly outward and try to expand its influence, not only into Cambodia and Laos but beyond?

Will Sino-Soviet competition in the Indochina area limit the influence of both, or will it stimulate both to step up their interventions politically, and even, conceivably, militarily? Will the Indochina states wish to develop significant contacts with the United States and Japan, or will they try to keep them at a distance? Will intra-Communist rivalries in the Indochina area impose restraints on Peking and Hanoi in supporting insurrectionary movements in adjacent noncommunist nations, especially Thailand, or are they likely to increase their support? Will Hanoi try to check the growth of Chinese influence in nearby areas of Southeast Asia, or will China limit Hanoi's influence, or will they eventually act jointly to expand Communist influence?

Will the new situation accelerate trends toward regional cooperation among the noncommunist nations of the area, or will the new pressures result in even greater fractionalization? Will friendly contacts develop between them and the Communist nations within the area, or will the trend be toward two hostile blocs? Will the noncommunist countries of Southeast Asia be able to deal successfully, and in a balanced way, with all four of the major powers in East Asia, or will they be subjected to growing pressures to align with one external power or another?

It may be years before answers to all these questions emerge. The answers, which will shape the future of the region, will depend on the policies pursued both by the Southeast Asian nations themselves and by the major external powers. Today, several trends seem probable. It is likely that most nations within Southeast Asia will stress increased self-reliance and the need for regional cooperation to prevent military intrusions by the major powers and will try to maintain friendly relations with all four of the major East Asian powers. They will probably try to avoid large-scale military conflicts among themselves in order not to provoke new big-power interventions. The major powers, in their varied political and economic involvements in the area, will probably tend to balance and restrain each other.

It is highly unlikely that any power, internal or external, can achieve dominance in the area in the foreseeable future. The atmosphere is likely to be intensely competitive, but essentially politically and economically rather than militarily. Insurrection will continue to be a problem in many of the noncommunist countries, its seriousness increasing or decreasing as the support Peking and Hanoi give the revolutionary movements varies (for Thailand this problem could be particularly acute and immediate). Success in coping with revolutionary pressures will depend above all, however, on the effectiveness of these governments' domestic political, economic, and social policies, rather than on external factors. However, they should be able to reduce external pressures if they are successful in establishing new relationships with Peking, Moscow, and Hanoi, while continuing to maintain good relations with Washington and Tokyo.

The changes in both American and Chinese policies in the late 1960s and early 1970s were fundamental factors helping to create the new situation. The U.S. decision to withdraw from Vietnam, and Peking's subsequent adoption of a more tolerant view toward U.S. activities elsewhere in Southeast Asia, made possible the end of the Sino-American confrontation by proxy that had previously dominated the situation.

However, Washington and Peking still view each other with ambivalence, in Southeast Asia as elsewhere. Both see certain parallel interests, yet each continues to regard the other as a long-term adversary, albeit a limited adversary.

The priority immediate objective of Peking's policy toward Southeast Asia appears to be to prevent any other power from acquiring a position there that could either pose a direct threat to China's security or gradually diminish Chinese influence. There is almost no evidence that Peking harbors far-reaching expansionist aims, in a territorial sense, in the area. While Chinese leaders may hope to convert the area into a Chinese sphere of influence eventually, their policies suggest that they recognize that this is not a practical immediate objective. The emergence of Vietnam as a strong middle power may make it seem less feasible even in the long run. China's present leaders unquestionably favor the spread of Pcking-oriented revolutionary movements in Southeast Asia, but they obviously look on this as a very long term objective; and they do not appear to believe that revolutions can be effectively exported by Chinese troops. To date, they have cautiously limited even their covert support to insurrectionaries abroad, generally muting their calls for revolution in countries where they are actively fostering state relations.

Peking clearly views the Soviet Union as the main threat to its interests in Southeast Asia today. Recognizing that multipolarity demands a new Chinese strategy, it now sees positive value in the roles that the United States and Japan play as counterweights to Soviet power. Hence, its relaxed view of Japan's growing economic power in Southeast Asia, and its desire that the United States stay involved in the area, even militarily.

The United States obviously should welcome China's decision to de-emphasize U.S.-China conflicts of interest in Southeast Asia. And it should acknowledge a parallelism in the American and Chinese interest in limiting Soviet influence. However, this should not obscure the differences that continue to exist in the basic motives and long-term goals of the two countries.

Washington should be prepared, in parallel with Peking, to use its influence actively to deter any increase in Soviet military activity in Southeast Asia, or Soviet political interventions or subversion that could be destabilizing. Partly for this purpose it should continue to maintain a U.S. naval and air presence, at a reduced level, in or near the area. However, the United States should not, as Peking does, oppose all Soviet political and economic activity or influence in the area. A gradual increase in Soviet diplomatic ties and trade would not necessarily pose new dangers and might even be desirable in the context of a four-power equilibrium. As elsewhere in East Asia, the premise of U.S. policy should be that all four major powers can be expected to play significant roles and that the problem is to maintain a viable equilibrium among them.

The United States should continue to make clear its opposition to any incitement to revolution in the area, by Peking, Hanoi, or Moscow, and it should continue to provide support for noncommunist nations' efforts to combat both internal and external Communist subversion. It should make clear to Peking that U.S. policies toward both China and

Southeast Asia assume there will be no sudden increase in military or subversive threats to noncommunist nations in the area, and that if there were, the consequences for U.S.-China détente could only be harmful.

In general, however, despite the inevitable linkages between U.S. policies toward China and Southeast Asia, the "China factor" should be viewed now as a secondary rather than primary determinant of policy toward Southeast Asia. Even though the danger of U.S.-China conflict in the area has greatly declined, there is little prospect of genuine U.S.-China cooperation in dealing with most of the problems in Southeast Asia. Washington must deal with most problems facing Southeast Asian nations primarily on their own terms, therefore, and not simply as corollaries of its relations with the other major powers.

In Southeast Asia, as elsewhere in East Asia, the general goals of U.S. policy should be to reduce the dangers of conflict, enhance the prospects for international cooperation, support economic growth and development, and promote both equity and stability. Here as elsewhere, however, the United States must accept that its capability to shape events is limited, as is the capability of the other powers. Nevertheless, it should recognize that continuation of an active U.S. role is both desirable and possible, and can have a significant influence on future trends.

In pursuing its goals in Southeast Asia, Washington must now rely primarily on development of closer political and economic ties and deemphasize its military role, but it should not withdraw its military presence totally from the area. With the demise of the Southeast Asia Treaty Organization and reduction of the U.S. military role, it should strongly discourage other powers from increasing their military presence in the area. A minimal U.S. base structure should be continued, probably restricted to whatever naval and air installations the Americans and Filipinos can mutually agree are desirable, although if the Thais wish to negotiate standby arrangements for certain bases in Thailand, the Americans should be prepared to consider such arrangements. Washington should continue providing military assistance to noncommunist nations that clearly need it, mainly through commercial sales rather than grants, but it should restrict such aid if it appears to distort domestic political and economic development priorities or to be more significant in relation to competition among local elites than to national defense. It should also work to prevent local arms races in the area rather than supporting them.

While deemphasizing the military aspects of its policy, the United

States should work to expand its economic and cultural as well as political ties. It should provide more, and more effective, U.S. and multilateral development aid, reversing the recent decline in such assistance, supporting especially those programs and policies that stress equity as well as growth. Americans should applaud democratizing trends, and frankly condemn authoritarian tendencies, even in friendly countries. The United States should be unambiguous about its position, but it must accept the fact that its capacity to promote democracy in other countries is extremely limited.

The United States should endorse and support, by whatever means it can, steps toward increased regional cooperation in Southeast Asia. It should also welcome attempts to draw the Communist states of Indochina into these efforts eventually, and it should be prepared to support major development programs, such as the proposed Mekong River Valley project, that might further this aim. It should also encourage the establishment of varied diplomatic and economic links between the noncommunist and Communist nations, both within and outside the area. On its own part it should try to establish such links, as soon as it is possible to do so without unjustified political conditions set by either side. A basic aim must be to encourage new relationships that prevent the division of Southeast Asia into two hostile blocs. It should also do what it can to moderate the political competition among the Communist powers themselves, since heightened tensions between them might lead to competitive interventions. The simple fact of the United States' remaining active in the area and developing contacts with the Communist nations should contribute to this end.

In developing its policies toward Southeast Asia, especially in the field of economic aid, the United States should promote cooperative or parallel efforts with Japan. The Americans should not approve or support an unrestrained growth of Japan's economic role, however, since Japanese dominance could provoke strong political reaction in Southeast Asia and perhaps, eventually, in China. An important U.S. economic role in the area will provide Southeast Asian nations with options other than excessive dependence on Japan.

Looking ahead, the United States should support the goal, articulated by many Southeast Asian leaders, of creating a neutralized zone of peace, which, to be effective, would have to be buttressed by understandings or agreements among the major powers to respect it. This obviously must be regarded as a very long term aim rather than an immediate aim. A number of prerequisites would have to be fulfilled before it could be a realistic possibility. The first would be a strong consensus among the major Southeast Asian nations themselves on what neutrality involves and on the area the zone covers. A critical question will be whether the Indochina states can be included, for it is difficult to see how any arrangement to neutralize the area could be effective if the Communist nations remained outside the scheme. Another prerequisite, clearly, will be a consensus among the major powers in favor of the idea, and agreement on means to create confidence that they will accept whatever restraints are imposed on them, presumably including ones forbidding both the maintenance of military forces in the region and military intervention.

Difficult as it would be to achieve genuine military neutralization of Southeast Asia, it should be in the interest of all the major as well as local powers. It would clearly be consistent with both U.S. and Japanese interests assuming that it was dependable and did not allow Southeast Asian nations, even without big-power intervention, to threaten certain very important interests, such as transit rights through Southeast Asian straits. From the Chinese perspective, neutralization might seem a good way to minimize what they currently regard as the main danger to China in Southeast Asia, that is, military threats from Soviet forces. Peking has gone further than the other powers in publicly endorsing ASEAN, although what it might feel about a more specific proposal for neutralization would depend on its detailed contents—and on Peking's assessment of the regional balance of forces at the time. The Russians have been relatively cool to the idea, in part because they have tried to promote their own, even vaguer, concept of an all-Asia collective security pact, which, although Moscow denies it, clearly has an anti-Chinese motive behind it. But if broad support for ASEAN's suggestion developed elsewhere, Russian support would not be impossible to conceive.

In Southeast Asia, as in Northeast Asia, however, the intensity of Sino-Soviet hostility virtually excludes any possibility of meaningful four-power understandings in the near future, and without support from all the major powers, the idea of neutralizing the area has little prospect of coming to fruition. Nevertheless, the United States should hope that this will change, and it should publicly stress that, in its view, the neutralization of Southeast Asia, backed by agreement among the major powers, is a desirable long-term goal. At a minimum, taking this stand will clarify

U.S. motives and ultimate objectives, not only in respect to Southeast Asia itself, but also regarding the need for a more stable equilibrium throughout East Asia.

Global Economic Problems

In the years ahead U.S.-China interactions will obviously not be limited to the East Asian region, and U.S. policy toward China must take into account varied global problems—especially the economic problems that have become increasingly important to the entire international community in recent years.

Peking's policies as well as its official statements reveal that the Chinese now have a dual approach to world problems, which involves inevitable contradictions. On issues concerning China's security, relations among the major powers, or political developments affecting the global configuration of military power, Peking's policies appear to be shaped above all by realpolitik considerations and to be based on a balance-of-power strategy designed to strengthen worldwide opposition—by the United States, Japan, and Europe, as well as China—to the country Peking currently views as its "principal enemy," the Soviet Union. On such issues, therefore, the Chinese frequently see themselves as being on the same side of the global balance of forces as the United States.

In Europe, South Asia, the Indian Ocean, the Persian Gulf, Africa, and in fact almost anywhere that political and military relations between the United States and Russia appear particularly competitive or tense, and where the Chinese see dangers of Soviet expansion, Peking now tacitly or explicitly tilts toward the United States and pursues policies that tend to parallel or support U.S. positions. This has obviously worked to the U.S. advantage, since it has led Peking to deemphasize clashes of U.S. and Chinese policies in these areas and has resulted in a limited convergence of interests in certain areas. American and Chinese motives and long-term goals have continued to differ fundamentally, however; Washington's basic objective has been to reduce tensions and increase stability, Peking's purpose has been to manipulate and exploit contradictions.

On most economic issues Peking now defines its interests primarily in terms of a struggle by the developing Third World nations and revolutionary forces in these nations against the developed industrial world—and above all against the two superpowers. On these global issues the

Chinese generally view the United States as an adversary or target, even though they are often less harsh in criticizing Washington's policy than in attacking Moscow's.

Americans and Chinese therefore have frequently worked at cross purposes in recent years on global economic issues. The basic differences in their policies have been highlighted in many debates, at the United Nations and in international conferences. The details of these economic problems cannot be dealt with here since they are simply too numerous and complex. They concern such diverse matters as world food problems, policies on world resources (including oil), population problems, the management of international finance, policies on world prices, nationalization of foreign companies and control of multinational corporations, law-of-the-sea issues, international environmental problems, international communications and transportation questions, world health policies, and weather modification problems, as well as related problems concerning international organizations, peacekeeping, human rights, and the like. U.S. and Chinese positions have clashed on most of these issues. Relatively little serious research has been done on how these problems are likely to affect China's multiple interests and goals in the years ahead, how Peking's approach to them may affect the prospects for effective international action to solve them, and how Chinese attitudes and policies may evolve and change during the next few years. However, China's current official positions clearly challenge those of the United States.

Generally speaking, Chinese leaders, like many of the most militant leaders in the Third World, have blamed most of these problems on the allegedly colonialist or neocolonialist policies of "plunder and control" pursued by the economically advanced nations, and especially by the two superpowers. They have supported most demands put forward by Third World leaders for a massive and rapid transfer of wealth and economic power from the developed to the developing nations and a radical restructuring of the world economy to create a "new international economic order." Peking has urged Third World nations on the one hand to be self-reliant but on the other to strengthen cooperation among themselves in order to exert maximum pressure on the industrial countries. It has criticized most proposals for international solutions to economic problems put forward by the economically advanced nations. Its approach, until recently, has been to favor politicized confrontational policies rather than pragmatic attempts to compromise differences. This has made the United States and China adversaries on many issues.

On a number of specific issues, however, Peking's positions are more complicated than its general posture implies, and it has demonstrated that when China's own economic interests demand flexibility, it can modify its views; in practice therefore its policies sometimes diverge from its theories. Over time, moreover, Peking will probably be compelled to consider more seriously than it has the extent to which its own interests argue for greater participation in cooperative international programs.

Many contradictions and complexities characterize Peking's present policies, and various pressures could affect them in the future. Although the Chinese strongly support OPEC (the Organization of Petroleum Exporting Countries) and other international cartels, they show no inclination at present to join any of them. Despite their criticisms of most international activities controlled by the advanced nations, they have associated themselves with a number of international agreements and organizations that require broad cooperation—for example, ones dealing with transportation and communications—because they have seen that their own interests demand it. Even though they have encouraged Third World countries to advance far-reaching demands in regard to law-of-the-sea issues, including total control both over two-hundred-mile economic zones and over straits, they have hinted that they may be prepared to work out equitable compromises with their neighbors on use of the seas. Peking has not yet defined its own positions, however, and it still could decide to press for maximum Chinese gains in adjacent ocean areas by appealing to the principle of "natural prolongation of the continental shelf" rather than accepting a division of claims based on median lines.

The Chinese have publicly denounced most proposals for international cooperation in the field of population control, but their own birth-control programs are among the most vigorous of any in the developing nations; conceivably China may in time find it in its interests to involve itself in international cooperation in this field, despite all ideological and political inhibitions against doing so. While praising the world food conference for some of its accomplishments, the Chinese have so far opposed the idea of international cooperation to establish a world grain reserve system and to exchange information on agriculture. However, their own need for dependable access to foreign sources of food (which they currently are trying to meet through bilateral agreements) may eventually compel the Chinese to consider participation in worldwide efforts to solve food problems. Peking has strongly criticized the organization and policies of the World Bank and the International Monetary Fund, but it has made no move to join them, which it would have to do if it seriously wished to influence international financial policies (it has demanded, however, that the Bank and Fund expel the Nationalist regime's representatives). The Chinese may find it in their interest to participate more actively in cooperative international meteorological activities, if for no other reason than because China's weather could be significantly affected by major weather modification programs elsewhere, especially in Asia.

It remains to be seen whether China's overall policy will gradually move away from a confrontational approach on global economic issues toward a more flexible and cooperative approach. The signs of flexibility so far are still very small. During 1975, however, when many Third World and developed nations became more flexible in their attitudes and began to express a desire to develop a productive dialogue, Chinese statements also began to urge a dialogue rather than confrontation.

In recent years it has become increasingly clear to knowledgable Americans that, because of the rapid growth of international interdependency, global economic problems must be given a higher priority in U.S. policy than in the past. Events have compelled Washington to give greater attention to the task of defining new policies and programs, and creating new international institutions, to cope with these problems. It is also fairly clear that China's general approach to this range of issues has generally worked counter to U.S. goals.

In pursuing the general line they now support, the Chinese are obviously motivated above all by ideological and political rather than economic objectives. They appear to assume—perhaps correctly—that whatever economic costs their current approach may involve, these could be outweighed by political gains, especially in relations with the Third World. Because China is economically less involved in the interdependent world than any other major power, it can often assume the role of a bystander, encouraging militant positions by others, knowing that its own policies largely insulate it from the possible economic consequences of north-south confrontation.

The fact that China is not a major participant in the world economy also means, however, that on many issues, while it can speak fairly loudly and exert some political influence, its economic leverage is limited. On most issues it simply cannot play a decisive role, or determine how other nations (whether developed or underdeveloped) whose economic interests are directly involved will act. Consequently, even though Chinese policies are generally not helpful from the U.S. point of view, the basic problems Washington faces in dealing with these issues do not in any sense focus on China.

In its own approach to these problems the United States should accept the fact that it is both necessary and desirable to have greater Third World participation in international economic policymaking and recognize that significant real transfers of resources from the industrialized nations to the developing nations are called for. It should also commit itself to strive for greater equity in relations between the developed and developing nations. Together with the other developed nations, it should begin the difficult process of negotiating realistic solutions to the many problems facing both the poor nations and the rich nations. Washington has taken some steps in these directions, but clearly the process has just begun.

In approaching global economic problems, the United States should be attentive to Chinese views, but need not give them undue weight. On these issues, as on many others, the United States should try over time to persuade the Chinese that their own interests would be better served if they would place less emphasis on international "struggle" and more on multilateral cooperation. But it should not expect China's overall approach suddenly to change fundamentally. And it need not be deterred by Chinese criticism and opposition from pursuing policies that are, from the U.S. point of view, realistic and reasonable. In the immediate future, both the United States and China obviously can live with their differences on global economic problems, and there is no reason these differences should pose insuperable barriers to continued improvement of their bilateral ties.

However, the United States should make it clear to Peking that when the Chinese adopt uncompromising or uncooperative positions that could hurt their own economic interests, they must be prepared to accept the consequences. If it proves possible to establish a world food reserve system, for example, the Chinese must be made to understand that if they refuse to participate, they cannot expect to have access to grain supplies on terms equal to those who are participating, which could pose serious problems for Peking in a time of severe world shortages if China had pressing grain needs.

The U.S. should hope that in the long run Peking's leaders will decide that China should become increasingly involved in international economic intercourse, in ways that will serve its own interests as well as those of others, and should participate constructively in international efforts to solve global economic problems. As long as China, with more than a fifth of the world's population, remains out of the mainstream of international affairs, Chinese tendencies toward parochialism will be reinforced and the solution of many economic problems that require worldwide co-operation will be complicated. Because of the strong pressures still operating in China in favor of self-reliance, it will not be easy for Peking to move toward the mainstream of a world characterized by increasing economic interdependence. But until it does move in that direction, there will be very special obstacles to the development of genuinely close relations between China and any other major nation—including the United States.

V

An Approach for the Future

THE many problems that have been discussed above constitute an agenda of issues to be dealt with in U.S.-China relations not in the next year or two but over the next decade—or perhaps two or three. Under the best of circumstances it will take many years to reach agreement, or even to narrow existing differences, on many of them. On some, mutual accommodation could prove to be impossible for the foreseeable future, in which case they will persist as barriers limiting how far U.S.-China détente can go.

Obviously the United States should not try to raise all of these issues at once with the Chinese. The result would be to overload the relatively fragile relationships that now exist. In the formulation of China policy in the years immediately ahead, therefore, both questions of priorities and questions of timing will be extremely important. It will be necessary to decide what problems are most urgent or most feasible to deal with at any particular time. It will also be essential to view specific moves as part of a long and gradual process aimed at building the foundations for a stable Sino-American relationship.

It is not possible to look very far ahead in specifying the most desirable sequence of moves in building a stable relationship. All decisions, particularly about timing, will have to be made in the context of the time. It is possible, however, to make judgments now about what should be given priority in the period immediately ahead. First of all, the establishment of formal diplomatic relations with Peking—and the concomitant changes in U.S. relations with Taiwan—must be given high priority. The act of upgrading ties with China is not intrinsically of crucial importance, but it will probably be impossible to deal with many more important problems until this occurs; and unless it occurs, even the present minimal relationship between Washington and Peking might deteriorate. Once normal diplomatic relations have been established, further development of economic relations and cultural exchanges should be pressed, principally because it seems likely that some progress can be made in these fields relatively rapidly, thereby pushing the overall process of U.S.-China détente forward. Priority should be given to those two fields, in short, more because they are comparatively easy to deal with than because they are of great immediate importance per se to the United States.

The United States should also give priority to two other problem areas that will be extremely difficult to deal with. One is the problem of preserving peace and promoting détente on the Korean peninsula. The other is the problem of involving China in arms control measures, particularly control of nuclear arms. Though Peking may resist even discussing these problems, and though it may take years to reach agreement in these fields, the United States should give priority to these problem areas for the basic reason that they are of crucial importance to future peace and stability in the entire East Asian region.

As it attempts to consolidate and expand relations with China, the United States will have to make some difficult decisions on the extent to which it should link various issues, by insisting that progress in certain fields of particular interest to the Chinese require parallel progress in fields that the United States believes to be especially important. Any strategy that attempted to make too many linkages would be unwise, since it would almost certainly be a prescription for deadlock; many problems will have to be dealt with on an ad hoc basis. Nevertheless, the United States should insist that genuine improvement in U.S.-China relations requires two-way compromises. In many instances, therefore, it can legitimately demand that significant U.S. compromises that benefit Chinese interests should elicit concessions from the Chinese on issues the United States considers particularly important.

Broadly speaking, there is no doubt that progress or retrogression in any significant problem area will influence the overall state of U.S.-China relations, even if no deliberate steps are taken to link particular issues. Step-by-step progress in solving particular problems should result in a steady improvement in the overall relationship. However, the entire process could be set back, or even undermined, by serious clashes of major interests which called into question the basic intentions of either side or even by a less dramatic but general deterioration of relations. It will be important, therefore, to sustain a sense of momentum in the process of building a new relationship, no matter how gradual the process may be.

In approaching the task of building a basis for viable and lasting relationships with the Chinese the United States must recognize that China—even more than most countries—is tremendously influenced by its past. It must take fully into account the fact that China is in the midst of a prolonged transition, some aspects of which can be traced back more than a century and others of which are very contemporary. In important respects, the Chinese have been moving toward a posttraditional, post-revolutionary, and post-Maoist era. This greatly complicates both the problems the Chinese themselves face and the problems that others will face in dealing with them. It poses some very basic questions about the general directions in which Chinese foreign policy could move in the years immediately ahead.

Traditionally China viewed itself as the Middle Kingdom. It was largely a world unto itself, and its leaders tried deliberately to isolate Chinese society and resist all alien forces impinging upon it. Since China's isolation was shattered in the mid-nineteenth century, the Chinese have struggled to come to terms with the modern international system, just as the world community has had to try to come to terms with China. Even though Peking's international activities have grown significantly, the process of incorporating China fully into the international community is far from complete. Looking ahead, one must ask: will the Chinese move toward greater and more responsible participation in world affairs, or will they continue trying to protect their values and interests by keeping the world at arm's length? Clearly, the United States should do what it can to encourage broader and more constructive international involvements, and the policies that the United States and other nations pursue toward China will help to determine whether or not this occurs.

Since 1949, members of China's first generation of Communist leaders have been moved, in dealing with the outside world, in part by hard-headed calculations regarding China's security requirements and in part by their strong revolutionary vision. Their vision has demanded that they not just accept the international order as it is, but instead should call for sweeping changes in it. As a consequence, while most leaders of major powers today at least give lip service to the goal of a stable "world order," whatever their actual policies may be, Peking's present leaders still speak approvingly about the "great disorder" in the world, arguing that disorder today will help to create a new global order tomorrow. In reality, though, they have been impelled to accommodate gradually to the international system as it actually exists. As China moves into a postrevolutionary period, how will its future leaders view the international system? Will they, in time, throw their weight increasingly in favor of world order, or will they continue to call for revolutionary disorder? The answer to this question, too, will obviously be affected by the policies of the other powers, and one goal of U.S. policy should be to encourage China to opt for policies designed to contribute to a more stable as well as more equitable world order.

During the past quarter century, the dominant world outlook in Peking has also been distinctively Maoist. The impact of Mao's thought and personal style has been enormous, on Peking's foreign as well as domestic policies. Not only did Mao play a major role in sustaining the leadership's commitment to revolutionary ideals; equally important, his personal views were crucial in determining the regime's particular balance-of-power approach to the problem of dealing with the other major powers. Will this approach continue in the post-Mao period? Or will Peking, under new leaders and in new circumstances, view its security problems and overall objectives in different terms? As China's own strength and self-confidence grow, will its leaders feel less threatened by the outside world, and if so, will they no longer feel compelled to pursue hostile policies toward some "principal enemy"? Will they continue to pursue a manipulative balance-of-power strategy of the kind Mao prescribed, or will they accept the idea of an equilibrium among the powers as a desirable goal? Will they continue to emphasize policies designed to exacerbate and exploit "contradictions" or will they be prepared to adopt policies designed to stabilize conditions and reduce tensions? Broadly speaking, U.S. policy should aim at convincing China's new leaders that a dynamic but peaceful equilibrium among the powers is in their interest.

The answers to all these questions will be determined to a large degree by what happens within China in the years immediately ahead, but they will also be determined by the approaches that the other major powers adopt in dealing with China. Broad historical considerations such as these obviously do not point to easy answers to concrete, immediate policy problems. It is nevertheless important to keep them in mind when dealing with current issues.

Index

Agriculture, 36, 40, 42, 44, 46
American Committee on Scholarly Communication with the People's Republic of China, 44
American Council of Learned Societies, 44
An Miao, 12n
Arbitration agreements, 41
Arms control, 34, 51, 63–77, 86, 123; China's role in, 64–66, 67–71, 72; key issues in, 64, 66–67, 70; and SALT, 64, 67, 68; superpowers' proposals on, 69–70
Arms transfers: to Arabs, 59; to China, 56, 57, 60, 61, 62; to Europe, 62; to Korea, 101; to Southeast Asia, 113; to Taiwan, 26–27, 29, 31
Assets and claims, 40
Association for Southeast Asian Nations, 109, 115
Australia, 42, 106
Aviation agreements, 40
Authoritarianism, 102, 108, 114

Banking agreements, 41
Barnett, A. Doak, 2n, 11n, 64n
Biological warfare, 67, 69
Blum, Robert, 2n
Boeing Company, 45
Business, U.S.: and China, 39–40, 41; and Taiwan, 30, 32–33. See also Commerce

Cambodia, 5, 8, 107, 110
Canada, 42
Carter, Jimmy, 14
Central Intelligence Agency, 35n, 39n
Chemical warfare, 67, 69
Chen, Nai-Ruenn, 35n
Chiang Ch'ing, 10

Chiang Kai-shek, 9, 14
Ch'iao Kuan-hua, 65, 66
Childs, Marquis, 7n
China Council for the Promotion of International Trade, 45
China-Japan relations, 13, 32–33, 43, 52, 73, 87, 89–90, 92–94; and China-U.S. ties, 58–59, 63, 75, 77, 79, 90, 94; formal, 5, 40; and Soviet pressure, 89
China, People's Republic of: Americans visiting, 43, 44, 45–46; diplomatic goals of, 9, 19, 111–12; and disarmament talks, 64, 67–71; domestic policies of, 10–11; economic expansion of, 19, 119; foreign policies of, 3–4, 11, 12, 52, 67–69, 70, 103–04, 116, 118–19, 124; isolation of, 2, 120–21, 124; and Korea, 2, 13, 98, 100, 101, 103–04; military strength of, 25, 38, 52, 57, 61, 63, 86; National People's Congress, 10; national security of, 2, 3, 11–12, 20, 56–57, 69, 74, 83, 104, 115, 116; as nuclear power, 7, 52, 69; and oil development, 32, 36, 38, 44; regional power role of, 1, 6, 20, 21, 22, 26, 34–35, 38–39, 53, 59, 73, 75, 80–81; as Third World leader, 21, 70, 72, 116, 117, 120; and United Nations, 16; U.S. hostility toward, 1, 2, 3, 4, 19–20, 38, 74, 79, 84, 111; -U.S.-Soviet triangle, 21, 22, 38–39, 53, 54, 58, 59, 61, 62, 63, 68–71, 73, 84, 86–87; U.S. trade with, 6, 8, 34, 35–42, 44, 48; U.S. view of, 2, 3, 4, 6, 13, 48, 49, 52; -Vietnam relations, 105, 106, 107, 110. See also China-Japan relations; China-Soviet relations; U.S.-China relations
China, Republic of. See Taiwan
China-Soviet relations, 7, 11–13, 37, 38–39,

127